CW01619497

The Regional Military Histories

THE CENTRAL MIDLANDS

The Regional Military Histories

Editor   Philip Warner

Scotland
The North-West
The North-East
Ireland
The North Midlands
The Central Midlands
Wales
The South Midlands
East Anglia
The South-West
The South
The South-East

The Regional Military Histories

The Central Midlands

Worcestershire · Herefordshire · Shropshire
Warwickshire · Northamptonshire · Bedfordshire

Lt. Col. Howard Green

Osprey

Published in 1974 by
Osprey Publishing Ltd., 137 Southampton Street,
Reading, Berkshire

© Copyright 1974 Howard Green
All rights reserved

Picture research · Pat Hodgson
Series design · Behram Kapadia
Maps · Patrick Leeson

ISBN 0 85045 181 7

Filmset and printed by
BAS Printers Limited, Wallop, Hampshire

*For Betty Ryder
with our love*

Contents

ACKNOWLEDGEMENTS

Thanks are due to the following for their help in supplying illustrations or making their material available for reproduction:

H.M. the Queen, Aerofilms Ltd., the British Tourist Authority, the Cambridge University Collection, the Department of the Environment, Herefordshire County Libraries, the Imperial War Museum, the National Army Museum, the National Monuments Record, and the Radio Times Hulton Picture Library.

The cover picture is of Goodrich Castle, Herefordshire and is British Crown copyright; reproduced with the permission of the controller of Her Britannic Majesty's Stationery Office.

INTRODUCTION

THIS book is intended for three types of people. Firstly and primarily it is readily digestible for the keen historian-traveller who is willing to leave his selected route for the day on seeing a signpost marked 'Naseby' or 'Mortimer's Cross'. This book will take him over the battlefield and fill in the events leading up to that historic event. With him may be a companion, studying the map, whose curiosity too may be roused on seeing the cryptic sign of crossed swords and a date. For some readers it may create a desire to see and visit these and many other scenes of early battles.

Secondly it is for the more serious student whose appetite may be whetted by what he reads in this book. He already knows a lot about Evesham, Worcester, Tewkesbury, facts and theories he has learnt in the study or classroom. Now perhaps he will want to go out and see for himself the ground and features which are still there. Perhaps he may weave new theories about past events, or speculate on what might have happened had different courses been adopted.

Lastly there is the local inhabitant possessed of much *esprit-de-county*. He will be delighted to read about the military events of his own county especially if he is an old soldier (and there are few men today who were not in one of the three services or Home Guard), presented to him in a concise form. He will appreciate having it all put before him without having to visit the Public Library and dig it out for himself.

A good deal of space in each chapter is devoted to the prehistoric hillforts, Roman encampments, and Norman castles. Although the events concerning them are so far off in time, the features themselves are still here to see. Invariably they are well known locally and the local historian who is not very interested in any other county, will be glad to read about his own county and to get straight at last the local legends, stories, reputations he has heard since his boyhood.

Naturally considerable stress is laid on the famous battles that were fought in each county. It is hoped that the reader will learn that it was quite fortuitous that Simon de Montfort and Prince Edward met at Evesham in Worcestershire or Richard III and Henry VII met at Bosworth in Leicestershire. Few of the great engagements in this book had any county connection but all were fought in, or for, England. The local countyman will consider himself lucky that the battle brought and still brings visitors, pilgrims, and trade to his town, while historians regard each, primarily, from the convenience of reaching the site.

A good deal of attention has been devoted to the local regiment. Every county has an intensely strong link between itself and its regiment, and no other country in the world has anything approaching this county spirit. However, only one or two incidents from each regiment's history have been dealt with owing to the limited space available. On one or two very rare occasions the strict county boundaries have been crossed, to include a military event that was very near. Usually a rigid rule to stay within the county boundary has been observed.

SHROPSHIRE
Ellesmere
Oswestry
Wem
Market Drayton
Newport
SHREWSBURY
Wellington
Severn
THE WREKIN
Much Wenlock
THE LONG MYND
Church Stretton
WENLOCK EDGE
Bridgnorth
Bishop's Castle
CLUN FOREST
Clun
Craven Arms
Stokesay
CLEE HILLS
LUDLOW
Teme
Sutton Coldfi
BIRMINGHAM
Stourbridge
W
Kidderminster
CLENT HILLS
Bewdley
Stourport
Bromsgrove
Redditch
Upton Warren
Henley Arden
Droitwich
WORCESTER
Alceste
Mortimer's Cross
Pembridge
Leominster
Kington
Weobley
Bromyard
Powick
Great Malvern
Avon
Evesham
HEREFORD
Wye
Madley
Ledbury
St Devereux
Pontrilas
Ross-on-Wye
Goodrich

The Central Midlands

Invaders from the Continent dig themselves in: Iron Age hillfort on Bredon Hill, Worcestershire. The largest and most magnificent survival of the Western Frontier of England – an attempt by succeeding invaders to contain the retaliatory raids of the Welsh. *c*. 700 BC.

WORCESTERSHIRE

UNTIL somewhere between 6000–5000 BC the two British Islands were joined to the Continent from approximately where Scarborough stands today round to Beachy Head in Sussex. Over the vast plain of the Netherlands, Northern France and what is now the bed of the North Sea, numberless tribes roamed around and across the low-lying lands. Virtually savages, naked in the summer and only just able to feed themselves by hunting, they knew no frontiers or boundaries and the passage of several millennia left them almost as uncivilized as when the great Ice Age ended about 8000 BC.

Then the northern ocean and the English Channel, greatly swollen by the melting and retreating ice in the north, broke through the narrow shallow valley and linked to become what is today the Straits of Dover. At once Great Britain became an island and the tribesmen cut off by the new water became an island race.

The Europeans on the southern side of the channel remembered the fertile pasture lands, forests containing so much game, and the mild winter climate of the new islands, and they made countless raids across the North Sea, the Straits, and the Channel.

Because Britain consists of two physical regions, the lowlands of the east and south and the highland zone of the west and north, incursions, both peaceable and warlike from the Continent, all pursued the course which every invader of the island has followed since.

Driving back the marooned English, the foreigners, usually Celtic from around the low countries of north-east Europe, fanned out to the west and north, until the successive waves of invasion finally broke on the eastern-facing escarpment of the Malvern Hills, and the eastern slopes of the Cambrian Mountains. Already wearied with penetrating the Worcestershire forests, and the marshy Severn Valley, they now faced the mountain fastnesses of the Welsh. Here they came to a halt. It is certain that many country people in Worcestershire, Herefordshire, and the Severn Valley today have Saxon, German, Flemish or even Roman blood in their veins.

For many centuries and despite repeated assaults by these Continental invaders, followed by Romans, Norsemen, Danes, Saxons, and Normans it was not until 1282 that Edward I finally subdued the Welsh. The people left behind when England became an island, were the original inhabitants before the joining of the waters and, pushed back into the mountains and intermarrying with the Welsh, remain the purest bred people in Great Britain today, having little Roman, Scandinavian or Norman blood. Indeed Worcestershire, Herefordshire and Shropshire might well have been called the Western Frontier of England after the formation of the islands.

Beginning of Worcestershire's military history

The earliest surviving signs today of military events in Worcestershire date from the beginning of the Iron Age – about 700 BC. The outline of several of their hillforts, constructed by Iron Age invaders from the Continent to hold a defensive line against the retaliatory raids by the Welsh, are still easily seen.

The largest and the most magnificent is on Bredon Hill between Tewkesbury and Evesham – which is best approached by car from Tewkesbury, and then through the villages of Kemerton and Overbury.

Bredon can be matched by the fortress on Herefordshire Beacon in the Malvern Hills, a climb of 600 feet from the Little Malvern–Ledbury Road.

This fort is particularly interesting as it shows the breach in the defences made at its weakest point, facing west, probably by a strategem of the Romans, who, knowing the defenders were looking to the east, assaulted it from the rear.

Similar camps, though smaller or less well preserved, are on Midsummer Hill two miles south from Little Malvern (take the A438 road from Tewkesbury. There is an easy walk of about half-a-mile from the village of Hollybush.) There was a fort at Hanbury Hill, four miles east of Droitwich but it has disappeared under the plough.

Opposite Holywell and British Camp from Worcestershire Beacon.

Ancient camp at Overbury, Worcestershire.

The Romans at Eastnor

History, as we know it, begins with the coming of the Romans in AD 43. Four years after their landing in Kent, they too had reached the Severn and come to a halt. Ahead of them they saw the line of hill forts built by their Iron Age predecessors whose descendants were still in occupation. But these forts now faced the wrong way, and the occupants had to re-orientate them to meet the new Roman invader. The Romans decided against a frontal attack and endeavoured to encircle the line by a flank manoeuvre up the Wye Valley. They partly succeeded, but the original invaders fought on and it was not until AD 78, thirty-five years later, that the Romans could advance into Wales.

It must not be imagined that the Roman invasion conquered England in five or six years. Certainly they occupied the country but not for many years did they conquer it. The warlike tribes, an amalagam of both overseas invaders of the Iron Age and the original natives, the English, would not give in to the Romans and risings of many tribes occurred during the first 150 years of the occupation. One was led by Caractacus, a Kentish chieftain who had fled to the west. He collected many local tribes to resist the new overlords, and in fact, kept his considerable army intact along the Welsh border for six years. However, he was eventually defeated in AD 50 by the Roman general Ostorius and, escaping with his life, reached the north where he was treacherously handed over to the Romans. He was defeated at Eastnor.

The battle of Eastnor ended the resistance of the English but the exact site of the battle is not known. As the Romans came up the Wye Valley it seems that they took Caractacus by surprise in the Malvern Hills to the west of Midsummer Hill. Turning to face his enemy, Caractacus probably moved along the high ground in Eastnor Park and then down to where Eastnor Castle stands today.

Peace descended upon the county until AD 583, when Worcestershire was invaded by the Saxons, a new enemy, since the Romans had left in AD 415. The Saxons settled in the Severn Valley, and absorbed the English, the Iron Age invaders and the Romans who had been left behind, or they were absorbed themselves. In AD 876 the Danes, having landed in Essex, also moved westward but after much manoeuvring, raiding, and minor clashes with the Saxon occupiers were driven back to the east by Alfred the Great, and the country again sank back into more peaceful living. It is noteworthy that many of the village churches in west Worcestershire have Saxon foundations and in a few cases Saxon walls and windows. But other than Eastnor, there are no exact records of the sites of the clashes between the Saxons and their original enemy, or later between the Saxons and the Danes.

William the Conqueror fortifies the border

The Norman Conquest did not greatly affect Worcestershire at first. However, the taking of the Domesday survey showed William I that there were many Saxon-English landlords along the Welsh border, all-powerful and a potential danger of an alliance with the Welsh against himself. Consequently he dispossessed many of the owners of the great estates and put his powerful Norman supporters in their places, encouraging them to build keeps as their headquarters. These were turned into defended castles, and so William, at the expense of his friends and kinsmen, had a line of fortresses from the mouth of the Wye to the Dee, against the incursions of the Welsh. Indeed during the 1800 years between the arrival of the earliest invaders from the Continent about 700 BC to the end of the Norman Conquest a broad band some thirty-five miles wide running northward from the Severn at Chepstow to the Dee at Chester contained more than forty castles, hillforts, prehistoric defensive ditches, fortified manors, guarding the avenues of

Eastnor Castle, Herefordshire. Restored and enlarged in the nineteenth century, the castle stands on the site of the battle (*c.* AD 50) in which Caractacus, last leader of the English resistance, was finally defeated by the Romans.

Birtsmorton Court. Elizabethan domestic buildings on earlier moated foundations of a typical fortified manor such as William the Conqueror's Norman supporters built to hold the Anglo-Saxons in check.

approach from the west. They were occupied time and time again down to the Middle Ages. Paradoxically the oldest of these defensive works are usually the best preserved and easiest to examine, while most of the fortified manors have disappeared or at best are only a shapeless mass of turf-covered rubble. However, in Worcestershire, castles at Birtsmorton near Tewkesbury, Wincherford Court near Worcester, Holt Castle near Droitwich, Chaddesley Corbett, Hartlebury Castle, and Dowles Manor all near Kidderminster, and Harvington Hall near Chaddesley Corbett, all show signs of Norman foundations or are on the precise original sites. There are, of course, others farther west in Herefordshire.

Holt Castle has the most to show and still has its Norman tower and hall. Holt Castle, Hartlebury, and Havington are open to visitors in the summer.

Another great and historic house not to be missed is Tickenhill Manor in the centre of Bewdley. Although of no direct military connection with Worcestershire, it is of historic interest in that here Prince Arthur of Wales, eldest son of Henry VII, was married by proxy to Catherine of Aragon in the chapel of this great house. It was a curious ceremony for the bride and bridegroom had never met, the bride was still in Spain and her marriage vows were taken by a Spanish nobleman, holding Prince Arthur's hand. They were eventually united in St Paul's in London but their married life was a short one as three years after the marriage Arthur died. His body rested for a night on its way from Ludlow to Worcester, in the chapel where the original ceremony had taken place. This marriage was to lead eventually to the break with Rome, the Dissolution of the Monasteries, and the unhappiness of three royal women and the execution of two others. (Charles I was staying in the house when he received the news of the Royalist defeat at Marston Moor in 1644. It is now a museum, open to the public.)

Woodbury Hill

Worcester City itself calls for a lengthy stay. Roman coins and other relics have been found, mostly underneath the Castle mound, but no traces of buildings or foundations have been uncovered. Nevertheless, Worcester's very name implies a Roman Castle and what better site for such a defensive work then opposite the ford which undoubtedly existed before the Severn was bridged. During the winter, and after heavy rain, the river must have been unfordable and tactically Worcester was a bastion against the Welsh should they penetrate so far east. In fact they never did pass east of Worcester. The nearest they got was in 1405 when Owen Glendower and some French mercenaries advanced against Henry IV. Henry held the Abberley Hills with a strong point on Woodbury Hill where the prehistoric fortifications were reoccupied. These fortifications can still be found although much overgrown with thorn and elder. The best way, the only way, up Woodbury Hill is from Lippetts Farm immediately south. A 400-yard walk will end at the fort. An interesting fact about this fort is that its steepest, and thus most difficult, side faces to the east, indicating that it was one of the earliest and built by the first 'Welshmen'.

After several weeks of minor skirmishes in these hills, the biggest of which was around where the eighteenth-century Hundred House now stands on the A443 Ombersley–Great Witley road, the Welsh withdrew. They had achieved nothing more than to threaten Worcester, and so Woodbury Hill has its place in English history as the farthest point ever reached by an invading Welsh army.

When Henry I, the last of the three Norman brothers to rule England, died he nominated his daughter Matilda as his successor. But the great barons considered a woman unfit to rule, and offered the crown to Stephen, nephew of Henry I and grandson of the Conqueror.

Stephen was a mild, pleasure-loving, easily-led man, with no good claim to the throne compared with Matilda, who was obviously the nearest to the succession. As a result there were 'nineteen long winters' when the able, dominating Matilda led many of the barons, who believed in primogeniture, against Stephen to win her lawful crown. Stephen was supported by those barons who did not believe a woman capable of ruling, and incessant marching and counter-marching between the two sides resulted. There was no spirit of a great crusade in either of the contestants but rather many barons and their armed tenants, seizing the chance to assault other baronial armies.

On one occasion King Stephen led his forces through Worcestershire to besiege Dudley Castle, and soon after Queen Matilda's troops sacked Worcester itself. Its Governor, Lord Waleran, had been created Earl of Worcester, but being absent from his post when it was sacked promptly deserted his monarch and went over to Matilda. As a reprisal Stephen plundered and burnt Worcester yet again.

THE BATTLE OF EVESHAM

The years between the Norman Conquest and the signing of Magna Carta in 1215 were an outstanding era in English history. It was comparable to the period from the commencement of the Stuart rule of eighty-two years when the religious dictatorship of the monarch flourished and was finally overthrown, to the bloodthirsty Wars of the Roses when so many leaders of England, both royal and aristocratic, lost their lives in battle, or by murder. (In twenty-five years twelve 'royals' alone died violent deaths.)

In the Norman period England was at last united under one monarch, and was ruled by a strong and generally fair dictatorship. But the quality of government gradually sank from its original efficiency and in the reigns of Stephen (1135–54), and Richard I (1189–99) became far from effective. Indeed Richard spent less than a year of his ten-year reign in England, being abroad pursuing his favourite interest, the Crusades. In his absence monarchy and firm central government became decreasingly effective and to many people appeared almost non-existent.

Richard I was succeeded by his youngest son, John, who had few redeeming features. He was a powerful, able, profligate, domineering character, and determined to rule as, for his own selfish ends, he wished. His malefactions, stupidities and cruelties finally so exasperated the great barons that in 1215 they forced him to sign Magna Carta, the cornerstone of Englishmen's – and Americans' – personal liberties today. On his death he was succeeded by his son Henry III.

Like many ineffective and weak men, Henry tried to hide his insufficiency by a superior, aloof, manner, a pose that infuriated the barons, all of whom were aristocrats. In addition he at once began to erode Magna Carta, the very terms of which the barons had forced upon his father. England was again falling under a dictatorship.

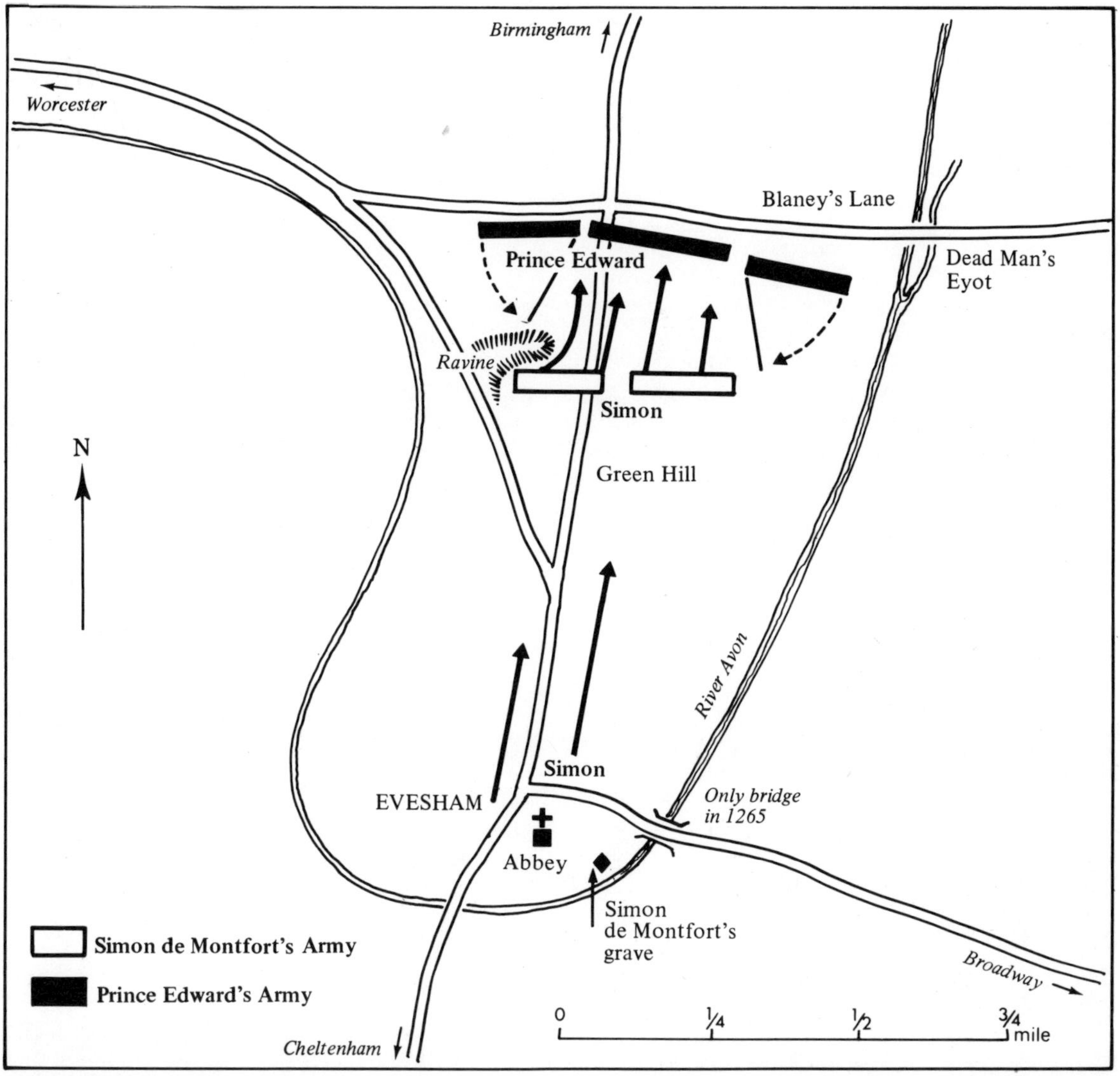

The Battle of Evesham

Simon de Montfort

In 1257 Simon de Montfort, a brilliant, able, very religious Frenchman, had settled in England. Being well-born he reached the court, married the king's sister, and quickly became Henry's chief adviser. But after a while he rebelled against the growing dictatorial methods of his brother-in-law, and the frequent repudiations of the charter. Accordingly he joined sides with the barons to restore such democracy as the Great Charter had created.

By 1260 the barons were so exasperated by the king's whole attitude to the law that they unanimously elected de Montfort to lead them in support of the rights of the people, and to declare war on the king.

In 1264, Simon marched against the king on Lewes Downs in Sussex and defeated him, taking Henry and his son Edward prisoner. He assumed complete power and took perhaps the greatest step any politician has ever taken in this country. He called together in 1265 a 'house of commons', consisting of members elected by their fellows from every shire and town, to sit with the great nobles as 'parlement' in Westminster.

Soon after the new 'parliament' had assembled, little Prince Edward, still a prisoner with his father in the hands of Simon, escaped and set up a Royalist headquarters at Worcester where he was joined by the gentry of Shropshire and Cheshire.

At the end of July Simon's army was in and around Hereford, King Henry still with it as a prisoner of war. At Kenilworth was his son, young Simon, just arrived from the south of England.

Prince Edward at Worcester on 3 August judged correctly that Simon senior would make for Kenilworth via Evesham to join his son. He decided to march southward to prevent a meeting of the two Simons and moved directly towards Evesham.

The barons under Simon de Montfort had reached Evesham on the evening of 3 August. Their march, over forty miles, entered Worcestershire at Little Malvern. They passed, of course, within two miles of the Iron Age hillfort on Midsummer Hill. Then through Upton-upon-Severn, where Cromwell commandeered the boats to bridge the Severn at the battle of Worcester about 400 years later, and then through Pershore, crossing the existing bridge over the town. His army must have been some 5,000 strong, mostly on foot, and doubtless created much sensation in the villages through which it passed. In the total absence of anything in the way of news, the peasants would wonder whether this large body of armed men meant trouble for them – especially as it contained a considerable contingent of Welshmen on whom the villagers in Worcestershire were accustomed to look with disfavour and suspicion.

The only bridge for Simon over the Avon in 1265 stood at the south-east segment of the great loop with which the river, flowing from the north, encircles the town, enclosing Evesham in its arms.

Simon senior and his army spent the night in the town, while their enemies moved into the mouth of the peninsula. Very early in the morning a look-out in the tower of Evesham Abbey reported troops forming up along the ridge running east-west across the main road about a mile-and-a-half out of the town. The Royalist forces were now concentrating all along the ridge immediately to the south of the modern second-class road running east and west across the Evesham-Birmingham road at Twyford House.

The frontage held by the Royalists was 2,000 yards long, and Edward had no more than 10,000 men. It meant only one man for every five yards, a very thin deployment even for a single rank in the thirteenth century. Accordingly Edward posted two very strong detachments, probably 3,000 men each, on each side of the crossroads at Twyford House at the top of the ridge, the Earl of Gloucester in command of the right and himself in command of the left. These 6,000 men were holding about a thousand yards and must have been about five men to the yard, ensuring a great depth. The remaining 4,000 men were posted more thinly on the two outer flanks.

The king is held hostage

Meanwhile Simon's army was marching out of the town northward up Green Hill Road. Their departure was delayed for a while as King Henry, still their prisoner, was anxious to attend mass in the Abbey, and Simon, a very religious man himself, gave permission for the service to be held. The hour or so lost enabled the Royalist forces to complete their formations and to give the men a little rest, which they sorely needed.

As Simon rode up the long slope of Green Hill he could see – what he also probably knew – that both his flanks were completely blocked by the unfordable river. He could see the Royalist army motionless in its ranks along the crest of the ridge. He had recently heard that the bridge behind him, his only line of retreat, was blocked by a Royal detachment. He realized that a great victory or annihilation lay before him.

When about 600 yards short of the top of Green Hill he could see the full Royalist army. Along the ridge, apparently, stood an unbroken line of soldiers, several ranks deep, fierce, aggressive, and presenting an unnerving sight.

At that time it was the universal practice in battle for each army to be drawn up in lines facing each other, and then for one to advance headlong on the other. But Simon, at the sight of the menacing Royalist line, decided on a novel tactic. He resolved to attack in great strength the junction of the two Royalist groups about where Twyford House is today. He believed, not without reason, that he might well penetrate the unbroken line facing him.

He advanced with his cavalry, some two hundred horsemen, in front. Immediately behind them he placed his prisoner, poor King Henry III, and it is difficult to find a reason for placing him there. Had he escaped and galloped forward to his own Royalist army he must have given them great encouragement and been a rallying-point in the event of disaster. Such a valuable asset for the attackers would have been much better out of the way, safely in the rear. Perhaps Simon wanted to be rid of his embarrassing prisoner, and deliberately put him where he could without great difficulty escape. But Simon was far too good a politician not to see how adversely

Battle Wells Field, site of the battle of Evesham and (*right*) the well at the top of the ravine. Simon de Montfort's extreme left knew nothing of its existence and blundered into it, 'bunching' into a dense mass of horses and men suffering heavy slaughter when the Royalists repelled their charge and encircled them.

Henry's escape would affect him. Putting the King in this position is one of history's minor mysteries. Behind the cavalry came the bulk of Simon's army.

The treacherous ravine

Running up from the south-west is a ravine. With steep and deep sides in its earlier path up to the road it forms a definite obstacle to an advancing army and Gloucester, commanding the Royalist right-hand group, probably saw it and decided to lie up behind it.

Simon did not know of this ravine and his extreme left flank must have blundered into it just about where its head flattens out into a small bog, referred to as the 'well'. As a result his left group to the west of the road tended to 'bunch' to its right and cause a density of troops in the centre greater than had been intended.

About 300 yards before the ravine Simon's army halted. Here Simon gave his orders to his subordinate commanders and then the order to charge.

The impact of the mounted knights galloping over the almost level ground closely followed by the tightly-packed body of infantry, made more dense by the bunching from the ravine, was terrific.

It smashed its way into the Royalist lines, the front ones of which recoiled on to the rearward. But the latter held, and Simon's furious and excited men were immediately embroiled in numberless hand-to-hand, and horse-to-horse clashes and a confused melée developed. The noise of the clash of battle so unnerved the Welsh following up behind the English that they turned and fled.

Those uncommitted Royalist outer flanks now started to advance and wheel inwards. Edward, seeing the whole position, realized that he could by this joint inward manoeuvre entirely surround his enemy. This he easily succeeded in doing, the two outer wings meeting behind Simon, so creating a ring in which great slaughter was to take place. The greater part of Simon's army was killed or so badly wounded as to be left on the field where they were despatched in the evening by the Royalists.

The few that did escape got away eastward to the river down the present Blaney's Lane, trying to cross the bridge at Offenham. Here they were caught, slaughtered to a man and their bodies thrown into the river. The spot is still known as Dead Man's Eyot.

Opposite Last stand of Simon de Montfort at Evesham, where he was defeated and killed. From the painting by R. Caton Woodville.

The king escapes

King Henry was carried by the impetus of the great cavalry attack into the centre of the fighting and only saved himself by continually shouting – 'I am Harry your King. Do not kill me.' Luckily he was recognized and led off to the rear of the Royalist line where, amid great rejoicing, he rejoined his son, Prince Edward. Probably no man in history has ever breathed such a sigh of relief as Henry did when he reached the safety of the rearward Royal lines and the welcome of his son. At some unknown time Simon was killed and by 11 a.m. all was over.

In the long run, England was the loser. She had another nine years of the not very effective Henry III and she lost the services of Simon de Montfort, one of the greatest politician-leaders she ever had, a statesman of the quality of Cardinal Wolsey, William Pitt and Winston Churchill. An unseen consolation for England lay in the person of young Prince Edward, the victor of Evesham. He was a tower of strength to his father after 1265 until he himself succeeded to the throne in 1275 – to be perhaps England's greatest King, ruling for thirty-four years. By his personal integrity, high-toned private life and, not least, by his imposing and regal person he raised the prestige of the Crown to a new high level.

The battlefield today

A visit to the battlefield of Evesham is, *prima facie*, disappointing. Much of it is now covered with woods, orchards, a large private park with 'Keep Out' notices, and new houses standing in their own grounds. Perhaps less than a third can be examined.

Luckily the most important area of all, where Simon made his initial great attack on the Royalist line, badly denting it, is still open and is occupied by a vast market garden.

The 'well' at the head of the ravine does not in fact exist as such. There is however an uncharacteristic bog there about the size of half a tennis-court, covered in brambles, stunted bushes, very deep grass, undergrowth and weeds. The ground is very damp and it is dangerous to penetrate very far. The bog is easily found along a cart-track off to the left about 150 yards short of the cross-roads at the top of Green Hill Road. Just before reaching the bog the visitor is standing in the middle of the battlefield and is within a few yards of the great melée.

Two hundred yards in front, roughly where the present orchard starts, is the position of the right flank of the Royalist right group. From here the

The carillon tower in the parish churchyard at Evesham was built in 1530. About twenty yards to the south stood the great bell tower of the old Abbey from which Nick the Barber saw Prince Edward's troops massing.

The Museum, close to the Abbey, contains interesting relics from the Battle of Evesham.

Royalists advanced swinging left to close the trap behind Simon's army. The right must have passed along the northern bank of the ravine and within a few yards of where you will be standing.

If the very narrow and bad cart-track, Blaney's Lane, running east from the crossroads (it is this cart-track that forms the fourth arm of the cross) is followed for two or three hundred yards one passes out behind the rear of the housing estate, and the unexpected but pronounced declivity is seen. The track gets worse and worse but as it peters out Dead Man's Eyot can be seen across the fields.

Simon's terrible tactical blunder of crossing by the only bridge over the Avon into Evesham and thus placing himself on a tongue of land where he had little room to manoeuvre is very apparent from the map, and more so when the site is visited. Yet in the event this appallingly dangerous position had no effect on the battle whatever. It was all fought out in a few hundred square yards and had the river and the one bridge not existed the result would have been the same. Greatly superior numbers must have told, even had all other factors been equal.

Before leaving Evesham a visit to the great churchyard of the parish church should be made. Here stood the old Abbey of 1265, although today its foundations have disappeared. The site of the great bell-tower, whence Nick the Barber saw Prince Edward's troops forming up, can be accurately fixed, about twenty yards to the south of the present carillon tower, built in 1530. The original tower and Abbey were demolished in the dissolution of the monasteries by Henry VIII in 1539.

About fifty yards south-east of the present tower, and standing alone on the greensward, is a solitary granite block with a bronze plaque. It marks the approximate site of Simon de Montfort's burial after the battle. The precise spot is not known, but the visitor can be certain that he is within a few yards of the grave.

The granite block was erected in 1965 when the 700th anniversary of the battle was commemorated. It was unveiled by the Speaker of the House of Commons and dedicated by the Archbishop of Canterbury, a fitting tribute by our democratic Parliament of today to its founder of seven hundred years ago.

The war moves from Worcestershire

The protracted wars between York and Lancaster affected Worcestershire hardly at all. There were only two incidents indirectly connected with the bloody period between 1455 and 1485. One concerned Buckingham, Richard III's favourite, almost at the end of the wars. The Duke of Buckingham had been Richard III's favourite counsellor and friend. However, the murder of the little princes in the Tower so disgusted Buckingham that he broke with Richard and went down into the West Country to await the landing of Henry Tudor – Henry VII-to-be. Henry's ship was delayed by storms and the few supporters whom Buckingham had gathered began to realize their peril. Many deserted and he was forced to move back into Worcestershire. Heavy rain so swelled the Severn that he could not cross. Cut off from his few friends over the river he moved north to try and find a crossing and occupied the famous Woodbury Hill. Here more desertions followed and when the river went down he was virtually alone. Quickly captured he was taken to London, charged, very informally, with disloyalty to the king and, of course, executed without trial.

The other incident in the Wars of the Roses that affected Worcestershire was after Prince Edward of York had won the battle of Mortimer's Cross in Herefordshire in 1461. He made straight for London where he proclaimed himself King Edward IV. He naturally took the quickest route after his victory. The Yorkists having lost the two previous battles before Mortimer's Cross, this victory at last gave him great prestige and enhanced his claim to the throne. Speed was essential.

His route is not known but it must surely have been through Bromyard, Worcester itself and then Pershore, Evesham and Broadway before passing out of the county. He would need all the force and armed men he could bring with him, and a considerable cavalcade must have been seen riding hard for London through these towns.

From the end of the Wars of the Roses at the battle of Bosworth in 1485 until the outbreak of the Civil War in 1642, little or nothing of military importance or interest occurred in Worcestershire. These 157 years saw the county expand its trade, its smaller and bigger towns, its roads and general development, unmolested by military events. A brief account of the one exception to this long period of peace may, however, be permitted.

Gunpowder plotters

Many of the bigger and more influential families in the county were strongly opposed to the religious antics of Henry VIII and his marriages. They remained Catholic, and their fortunes, often their freedom, were much affected by the years of religious persecution during the middle Tudor era. However they remained faithful to the 'old religion' and were thus in indeterminate conflict with the expanding urban and commercial areas of development just across Worcestershire's northern border.

The Wyntours of Haddington, the Talbots of Grafton, the Littletons of Hagley, the Habingtons of Hindlip were all Roman Catholics, while Thomas Wyntour and his cousin, Robert Catesby, were so rabid in their religion and hopes for its restoration that they were prime movers in the Gunpowder Plot. The Plot however was given away by Mrs Habington, whose religious convictions were so strong that she treacherously betrayed her husband's friends. They all fled to Haddington (five miles east of Worcester) and thence through Hanbury (east of Droitwich) – Hagley – Stourbridge – and then just across the county boundary at Kingswinford to Holbeche House, Stephen Littleton's house, where the party was surrounded. Catesby was killed, his companions being captured in the ensuing struggle and later executed. The actual site of the considerable fracas was the forecourt of the house. It happened where the present sweep of the gravel drive in front of the house lies today. In 1605 the present drive was paved and enclosed by a wall. Holbeche House, an imposing and dignified Elizabethan country house, stands half a mile south of the Himley crossroads on the Kingswinford-Wolverhampton Road. It is in occupation today, virtually unaltered from 1605, except for the addition of one large room unseen from the front.

THE BATTLE OF WORCESTER – 1651

On the outbreak of the Civil War in 1642, Worcester declared for the king, and it remained loyal until the defeat of Charles II in 1651.

Most of the visitor's stay in Worcester City must surely be occupied in examining the battlefield of Worcester of 1651, the last battle of the Civil War, 'God's crowning mercy', according to Cromwell.

To approach it properly it is first necessary to review the general and political situation in England at that time.

After the 2nd Battle of Newbury in 1645 the king's two sons, Charles, Prince of Wales, and his younger brother James, were sent to Holland to live almost in exile. Immediately after the execution of his father in 1649 young Charles was proclaimed Charles II, King of Scotland, and invited to return and claim his throne. He landed in Scotland in June 1650, where he was proclaimed king in Edinburgh amid great rejoicing.

Charles II raises his own army

Cromwell, now the dictator of England, was determined to prevent the establishment of a monarchy in Scotland and believed that country should share in the fortunes of a republic. Accordingly he marched into Scotland with 16,000 men and utterly defeated the Scots at Dunbar. Despite their defeat and determined not to accept republicanism, the Scots crowned Charles at Scone, where he quickly raised an army of 16,000. Many of those who had escaped from Dunbar were in the new army and were anxious both to avenge their defeat and to expel the English, now in and around Edinburgh. Charles, however, decided to avoid an encounter, and with his untrained but enthusiastic army slipped between Edinburgh and Glasgow and entered England at Carlisle, where on English soil he was proclaimed king of England by Englishmen. He marched hurriedly on and in three weeks was in the city of Worcester. His reason for diverting from the direct route to his capital, London, was to draw the Welsh from their mountains to join his army. Their enthusiasm proved lukewarm.

Cromwell masses at Coventry

Cromwell followed at once, his cavalry under General Lambert covering 200 miles in four days. He ordered all detached forces, no matter how small, to concentrate at Coventry, there to await his arrival. The Parliamentary army began to close in, and by 2 September they were astride the main road from Worcester to London with 30,000 men. Charles's position was now very serious. His army, despite a few recruits from Wales, was no stronger than its original size and he knew that Cromwell had outlying contingents coming in. Time was on Cromwell's side and he deliberately blocked the way south towards London, and to the west into Wales.

At Worcester the river Severn runs north and south with the city on the eastern bank. Two miles to the south a considerable tributary joins it from

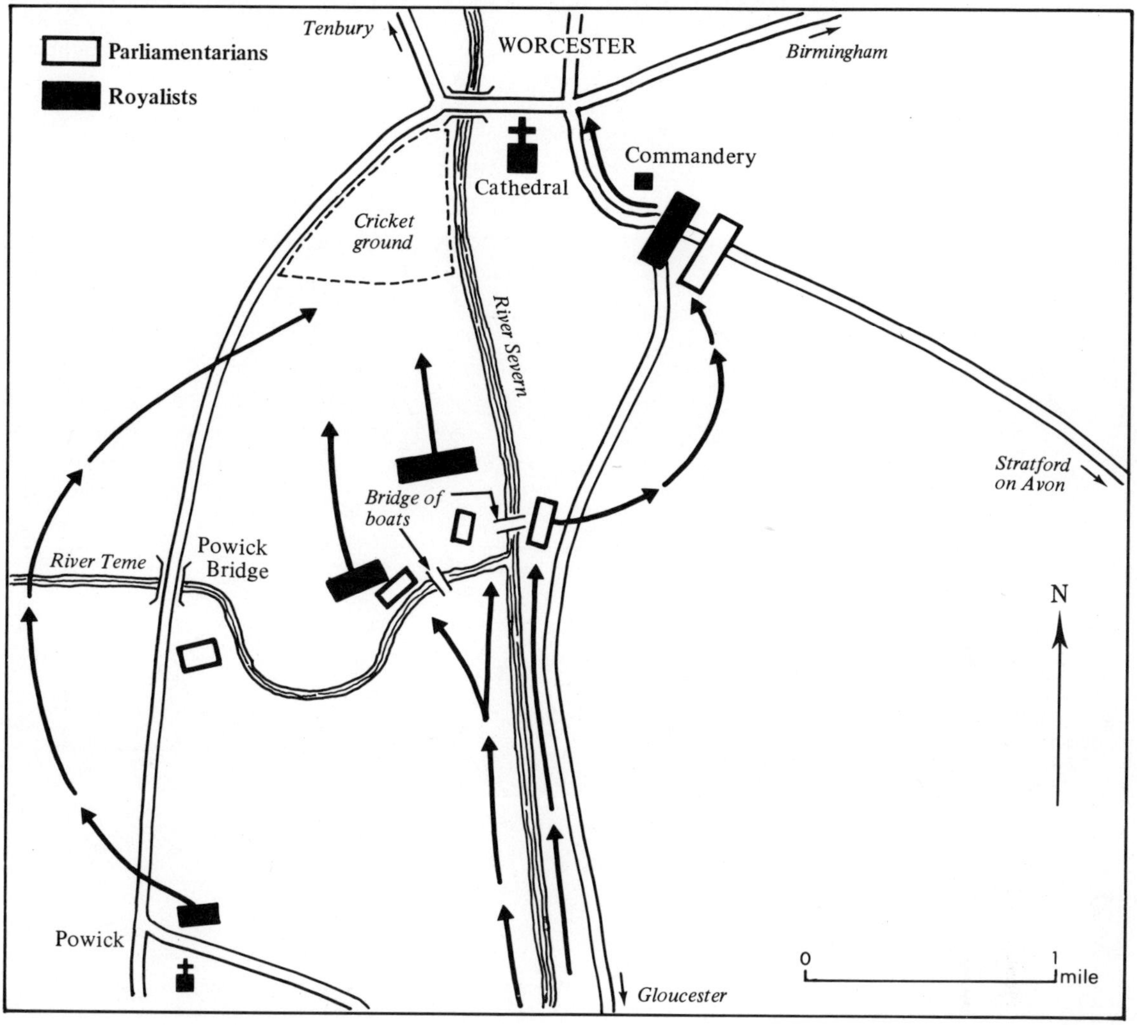

The Battle of Worcester

the west, the river Teme, thirty yards wide and with banks ten feet deep. It is full of salmon. The Teme is crossed by a bridge at Powick, a mile and a half before it joins the Severn, across which there was, or is, no bridge for eight miles below the city.

Next day, 3 September, was the anniversary of the battle of Dunbar, where the Scots had been decisively beaten the previous year. No doubt this fact depressed Charles's men, eighty per cent of whom were Scotsmen.

Oliver's pontoon bridges

That the only crossing of the unfordable Severn and Teme was at Powick, presented a grave problem to Cromwell. Accordingly he ordered General Fleetwood to cross the Severn at Upton, nine miles south of Worcester, and then commandeer some large flat-bottomed boats and tow them up-stream to near the junction of the two rivers. It must have been a gigantic task as the Severn here is fast and runs between deep, sheer banks. Fleetwood was given 11,000 men and of course all the towing had to be by manpower. Pontoon bridges were to be built across both rivers. The entire absence of opposition by the Scots troops lying in the meadows between the two rivers seems quite extraordinary.

A Royalist outpost across the river Teme was holding the village of Powick half a mile to the south of the bridge and there for a brief while held up the advancing Parliamentarians, who were to force the crossing of the Powick bridge (although it was damaged). The brief engagement in the churchyard

has left bullet-marks on the base of the church tower, which are clearly to be seen.

When the Royalist outpost withdrew Fleetwood's men came up to Powick Bridge, but owing to the damage only infantry could cross, the mounted men having to find a ford a mile farther upstream.

Meanwhile the towed boats had arrived near the junction. Five went up the Teme for a hundred yards and there started building, while fifteen boats went a similar distance up the Severn. Two bridgeheads were secured, to protect the bridging, by men ferried over in small rowing-boats to keep at bay any Royalist patrols. They were seen by one patrol which gave the alarm and reinforcements were sent from the city, but the two bridges were completed with little opposition; an astonishing feat. Cromwell led his men over the newly-built Severn bridge, joining forces with General Lambert, who had by now also crossed the Teme. They advanced together and gradually pushed back the considerable Royalist infantry force in the meadows between the two rivers.

Meanwhile, Charles from the cathedral tower saw the strong advance across the meadows below him, but also noticed that Cromwell's right wing was becoming isolated. It had the unfordable Severn between it and Cromwell's main operation, and was clearly vulnerable. Accordingly he collected all the horsemen he could muster (one Scottish cavalry regiment, Leslie's, refused to co-operate), and led them through the East Gate, now the

Opposite Powick: the churchyard in which the first brief skirmish of the Battle of Worcester took place. Bullet-marks are clearly visible on the base of the tower beyond the white cross.

Below Powick Bridge, near Worcester, where the Parliamentarians forced a crossing. Owing to the damaged state of the bridge, only the infantry could pass over it.

Above Worcester: Cromwell pinned by the ears, carved on the Guildhall.

Sidbury, against the slowly advancing Parliamentarian right wing. The Royalists quickly threw them back in disorder and, moving on, secured a good position on Red Hill, now a housing estate astride the A44 Worcester-Pershore road.

It was a critical moment but Oliver Cromwell showed his genius as a leader of men, as he had done at Marston Moor. Leaving Fleetwood in command in the meadows, to keep up the pressure, he galloped back over his pontoon bridge, followed by his successful brigade and, picking up his retreating right wing, led them back and with all his strength counter-attacked the Royalists on Red Hill. His leadership and iron will prevailed and the Scots were pushed off the hill, back through the Sidbury into the city. The Scots refused to stand and, although Charles rode up and down exhorting them, he could not hold them. Many threw down their arms and drifted away through the city, led by Leslie's horse. Meanwhile Fleetwood's advance

Left Worcester: the cathedral tower from which Charles II saw Cromwell's strong advance across the meadows where the County Cricket Ground is now.

Worcester: the Commandery. This Elizabethan building was the headquarters of the Royalist forces defending the East Gate. Here the Duke of Hamilton, commander of Charles's left, died of wounds.

across the meadows between the two rivers gathered momentum, and his force eventually pushed the Scots back to, and across, the present County Cricket Ground. Here the permanent bridge over the Severn was secured and all chances for Charles's army to escape west vanished.

Charles escapes to Boscobel Oak

Charles's English cavalry now stood fast, and to secure his escape charged back down the High Street and then the Sidbury. Held, and then forced back, they reached the Town Hall, where a last-ditch stand was made; they were eventually overcome. In the dusk Charles escaped to Boscobel Oak and after several weeks of hair's-breadth adventures he reached Shoreham Harbour and a boat for France. This famous oak is commemorated in over 400 public houses named 'The Royal Oak' in England today.

After 'God's crowning mercy', as Cromwell called his victory at Worcester, England was not again to be threatened by an invasion, Stuart or otherwise, to overthrow the throne, until Monmouth's abortive adventure over thirty years later, which ended at Sedgemoor.

The battlefield now

To visit the Battle of Worcester drive up the A4021 from Upton to Powick, to see the churchyard where the outpost skirmish took place, and the bullet-marks on the base of the church tower. Drive on towards Worcester, crossing the Teme by the modern bridge. Two hundred yards to the left is the old bridge, clearly showing portions of the original bridge before the partial rebuilding in 1837. Drive on, and the meadows up to the County Cricket Ground are on the right. Cross the Severn bridge and turn right.

Leave Worcester by the A44 Pershore Road, down the Sidbury. On the left of the road immediately opposite the turning to Kempsey is the Commandery, a very old building standing in 1651. It was the headquarters of the Royalist forces defending the East Gate, and where Charles collected the troops to attack Cromwell's temporarily weak right flank. It is a magnificent example of a large sixteenth-century town house. The main hall and the formal staircase are superb while the rooms upstairs should not be missed. After the battle many wounded from both sides were brought into this house.

Drive on down the A44 to the Ketch Inn, the only inn in England to bear this name. A walk back along the river bank for 500 yards brings one to where Cromwell's pontoon bridge was erected. The site of Fleetwood's bridge can be seen 300 yards away, across the confluence, and towards Powick.

THE WORCESTERSHIRE REGIMENT

The English have always disliked, almost distrusted, a permanent standing army. For many years they believed it to be the tool of the monarch to repress them by force, a fear that had been increased by Charles I's dictatorial methods. Even today a short Act of Parliament has to be passed yearly to authorize the Regular Army to remain in existence, and to be paid, for another year.

For a few years after the last battle of the Civil War, at Worcester in 1651, the New Model army remained alive, but the fear of the people of a renewed dictatorship by 1660 compelled the easy-going Charles II to disband the New Model. The last regiment to go, the Coldstream Guards, laid down their arms in 1661 and at once picked them up again as Charles's personal bodyguard. With only one battalion the Government realized that England must, of necessity, have some proper form of defence against an enemy from overseas, and authorized the raising of new regular regiments. By 1685 when Monmouth's foreign invaders threatened the country and were soundly defeated at Sedgemoor, fifteen new regular regiments had been raised and each succeeding year saw one or more added to the establishment, all of them to survive to the present day, although in some cases amalgamations have confused identities.

In 1701 the 29th Regiment of Foot started its career. After 160 years of continuous service it became the Worcestershire Regiment.

During the eighteenth and nineteenth centuries, the Worcesters saw service under Marlborough at

Night bivouac after the Battle of Ferozsah, 21 December 1845, in which the 29th Foot (Worcesters) took part.

Ramillies, in India, at Corunna, in the Peninsular War where it earned nine battle honours for its Colours. A long spell in India brought it five more battle honours.

In 1881 the 36th Foot, the Herefordshire Regiment, became the 2nd Worcesters and two more regular battalions were raised in 1900 to take the steady inflow of recruits from the rapidly expanding and near-by Birmingham.

In August 1914 the four regular battalions were stationed in Cairo, Aldershot, Tidworth and Burma, while the two Territorial Battalions, part of Haldane's totally reorganized volunteer force, were filled with excellent civilian soldiers in Kidderminster and Worcester, each having detached companies in smaller towns in the county.

The 2nd Battalion at Aldershot was in the 2nd Division and consequently took part in the Battle of Mons, the Great Retreat, the Marne and the Aisne, and then the 1st Battle of Ypres. This action of 1st Ypres is worthy of special notice.

1st Battle of Ypres

The Ypres Salient, occupied in mid-October 1914, extended originally around a sixteen-mile semicircle – with a radius of five miles out from the town. The Salient itself was held by the 1st and 2nd Division around Langemarck on the northern half.

The weight of the unceasing German attacks from 18 October onwards, fell mainly on the 7th Division astride the Menin Road, running south-east from Ypres. On 31 October the village of Gheluvelt was eventually lost and the Division had now been pushed back over a mile to its right rear. It was now entirely south of the Menin Road. That afternoon the South Wales Borderers, of the 1st Division, on the left of the 7th Division, holding the grounds of Gheluvelt Château, were under extreme pressure. A fresh German regiment had been brought forward and after several attacks had almost isolated the battalion from its respective neighbours, the Queen's and the Welch Regiment. Away to the right the Scots Guards, down to 200 men, were barely holding on and it seemed the line must break. If so the Germans would have passed through the 1st Division and thereby outflanked, overrun and defeated the BEF. The way to the Channel ports would have been open, the French left flank turned, and then – a rehearsal of the withdrawal to Dunkirk in 1940.

The 2nd Worcesters in the 2nd Division away to the left rear were in reserve, 'Standing to' in Polygon Wood, a mile away. To save the situation they were ordered to advance at the double across the open ground to reinforce the South Wales Borderers and prevent the imminent capture of Gheluvelt Château which stands some five hundred yards beyond the village.

World War I 4th Worcestershire Regiment returning from the trenches along the Albert-Fricourt road, 1916.

For the first six hundred yards the Regiment was under cover of woods on their left, but on reaching Polderhoek Château open country had to be crossed and for a thousand yards there was no cover of any sort. The first rush was for two hundred yards, and the enemy's shell and shrapnel fire naturally increased. Over a hundred men were killed or wounded out of the four hundred but the Regiment pressed on, reached the Château, there joining the South Wales Borderers. Some of the men, with the bit between their teeth, went on into the village (where they found some Germans in a ruined cottage cooking for their battalion. The cooks, though in vastly superior numbers, were so surprised that they turned and ran, while the few Worcesters returned to the Château).

'The charge of the Worcesters at Gheluvelt' was perhaps the finest exploit of any single battalion in the whole of World War I. It can only be challenged by the 1st Lancashire Fusiliers in their original

landing on the Gallipoli Peninsula, when that battalion earned six Victoria Crosses in one day.

The actual arrival of the Worcesters on the lawn of Gheluvelt Château in relief of the South Wales Borderers was the subject of a large oil painting, 'The Worcesters at Gheluvelt Château', which now hangs in the Headquarters of the Regiment's Depot at Norton Barracks outside Worcester.

The 4th Worcesters from Burma were posted to the famous 29th Division and so took part in the landing at Gallipoli in 1915. Here they fought at Cape Helles, Anzac and Suvla Bay, until in 1916 the Division came home to the Western Front. The Commanding Officer, Colonel Cayley, had, it is believed, a unique experience. Appointed to the command of the 4th Battalion in March 1914 in India he remained as CO until, in June 1915, he was promoted to the then vacant command of the brigade in which his battalion was serving. He remained as Brigadier until September 1917 when he was appointed Divisional Commander of the 29th Division and thus served for the whole of World War I in the same division. Such a four-and-a-half years' career, ending as Divisional Commander, is believed to be without parallel.

Recent history of the Worcesters

The two Territorial Battalions of the Worcestershire Regiment were part of the 48th South Midland Division in August 1914, a division with which they had served since Haldane's reconstruction of 1908. The two battalions took part in the Battle of the Somme (twice) the Advance to the Hindenburg Line, and Passchendaele (twice) and then went with the 48th Division to Italy in November 1917 where they remained until after the Armistice.

Sixteen new battalions of the Worcestershire Regiment were raised in World War I, of which nine went on Active Service.

The Worcestershire Regiment has never been a spectacular regiment, preferring to be quietly efficient, with no modern 'publicity'. As a result it has always been regarded as utterly reliable and indeed it has lived up to its Regimental motto, 'Firm'.

After World War I its two junior regular battalions, the 3rd and 4th Worcesters, were disbanded and the Regiment continued to serve with one regular battalion on Foreign Service, and the other in the UK. In 1939 the 1st Battalion was in the Sudan and after service there went on to Abyssinia, the North African Desert campaign, and then back to Europe for the invasion of the Continent on D-Day. The 2nd Worcesters remained in India from 1939 to 1945 when they took part in the Burma campaign against the Japanese.

The 7th and 8th Battalions, still in the original 48th Division of 1914–18, went out to France in 1939 and took part in 1940 in the evacuation from Dunkirk.

As in World War I, so in the second World War, new battalions were raised, two of which served overseas.

In 1946 the 8th Territorial Battalion was virtually disbanded but the 7th remained active and at full strength until 1967 – when it was reduced to TAVR status. In 1948 the 2nd Battalion was amalgamated with the 1st, as were the 2nd Battalions of all regiments. The 1st Worcesters soldiered on until, in the amalgamations of 1970 it joined hands with the Sherwood Foresters to become the Worcestershire and Sherwood Foresters. In 1973 it was in Berlin.

From Volunteers to the Home Guard

From the defeat of the Spanish Armada in 1588 the English had lived free from fear of invasion. For two hundred years there was no cloud in the sky that might endanger these islands. There was, it is true, much empire-building abroad in the eighteenth century requiring an army and a navy, but at home all was peace and apparently likely to remain so.

But in 1805 the British people suddenly realized that across the Straits of Dover Napoleon had massed 100,000 men with 2,000 flat-bottomed boats, all for a cross-Channel invasion of England. This sudden awakening to danger greatly shocked the people, and the great Volunteer movement sprang to life. Practically every town of any size and certainly every county raised a unit or sub-unit, all with their eyes across the Channel. Mostly paying for their own uniforms and rifles, they drilled enthusiastically on Saturday afternoons. Local gentry provided the officers and the lack of skill of the military training and discipline, sketchy though it was, was well hidden beneath the patriotic enthusiasm of all ranks. The units, all separate, with little higher organization than the battalion survived for over a hundred years and were to provide, in August 1914, fourteen Territorial Divisions in the First World War. These local units owed, in their earlier days, little allegiance to anyone other than their own town or county. They might be called the

Opposite Regimental badge of the Worcestershire Regiment. The motto, 'Firm', is under the lion.

HONI·SOIT·QUI·MAL·Y·PENSE
FIRM

Men of the Worcestershire Regiment with some Cameron Highlanders and the German lorry they commandeered and drove through the enemy lines in the escape from Tobruk, June 1942.

'Taunton Volunteers', or 'The Peterborough Rifles' or 'The Bolton Light Infantry', and not until late in the nineteenth century did these extremely independent units tend to drift into the orbit of the Regular Regiments, all of whom had in 1881 been allotted to specific counties and given county names. Many country inns today are still called 'The Rifleman' or 'The Volunteer'.

Worcestershire took its share of the Volunteer Movement manfully. In the first ten years from 1805, infantry units, sometimes only one company, were raised at Bewdley, Droitwich, Dudley, Elmley Lovett, Evesham and Pershore (this unit was over 400 strong), Feckenham, Tenbury, Worcester City (over 800 strong), and Kidderminster, with several smaller units. Cavalry was formed in Bromsgrove, Dudley, Kidderminster, Kings Norton, Stourbridge, and Wolverley.

The services of these units were at first confined to the county, but in 1813 their liability to serve elsewhere was raised although none in fact were called upon to do so.

On the collapse of the Napoleonic menace after Waterloo, interest waned. There were few recruits and most units only remained in existence by continuing as shooting clubs.

But in 1859 after the horrors of the Crimea and the Indian Mutiny became known, a great wave of enthusiasm again swept the country. New rifle clubs were formed and many moribund volunteer units sprang back into life.

By 1883 most units had undergone a phase of rationalization and amalgamated, forming the 1st and 2nd Volunteer Battalions of the Worcestershire Regiment. As such they sent parties of volunteers to reinforce the regular battalions in South Africa in 1900. In 1908 they became the 7th and 8th Worcesters, the 7th being still alive today, the direct descendant of the unit raised in Kidderminster 170 years ago.

Worcestershire raised twelve battalions of the

The Worcestershires' bivouac at 80-milestone Point, Imphal, November 1944.

Home Guard in the period 1940–5. Two were in Worcester City, with one complete company coming from the Great Western Railway, and another from the Post Office. The Goodyear Tyre Company at Dudley, the BSA and the Enfield Cycle Company, both at Redditch, each provided a battalion. A highly rural battalion was based on Great Witley, its headquarters in Abberley Hall; it had many small units in the villages around. One platoon from Bredon, in the 4th Battalion from Tewkesbury, had its miniature rifle-range in the Bredon Rectory garden, while the 7th Battalion in Malvern Link used the range at Malvern College. One company in this battalion came from the College, the masters and older boys from the fifth and sixth forms providing both officers and other ranks.

Some units, although compulsorily disbanded after the war, maintained their identity and cohesion by becoming rifle clubs. Twenty-six such clubs remained in existence for some years in Worcestershire alone, and in 1948 there were over one thousand members of these clubs in the county.

One very powerful element in the morale of the Home Guard of 1940–5 had been the realization that it would be fighting, perhaps dying, in front of its own people. They would be 'playing at home' and enjoying the advantage every home team has over the visiting team, no matter how powerful. It is believed that this sense of playing before the home crowd had much to do with the high morale of the young RAF pilots in the Battle of Britain. They knew they could actually be seen fighting, winning, sometimes dying, in front of their own people, an advantage denied to the BEF in its fighting withdrawal to Dunkirk, out of sight.

This high morale of the Home Guard was a unique feature in military history. Previously in history high morale had, at its base, discipline and training grafted on to an urge to defend and win, the most striking example being that of Kitchener's Army in 1914. The Home Guard in 1940–5 certainly lacked the drill and barrack-square training, and its weapon training and tactics were learnt under conditions far from ideal. Yet the urge to show the enemy, and their own families, their determination was so powerful that the spirit and the comradeship of the war years lasted on. The officers of one battalion of the Bedfordshire Home Guard still hold an annual dinner, and one small-town platoon in Cornwall has done even better. At Liskeard the order to 'stand down' in 1945 was ignored, the men not wishing to discard the comradeship or sense of belonging to a group. They continued to parade periodically in full view of the townspeople for some time after the end of the war and then, later, met together as a club in an old dance hall which they bought for £300. But membership inevitably declined as the years passed by through death, ill-health, or movement away from the town. Subscriptions consequently grew fewer while costs of maintaining the hall grew greater, and eventually the remaining members had to sell the hall, in January 1973, realizing that time rolls on. But memories will last.

HEREFORDSHIRE

MUCH of the story in the chapter on Worcestershire concerning the invasions over the English Channel applies equally to both Herefordshire and Shropshire, that story need not be retold here. Briefly, the invasions of England from 500 BC to 1066 followed a similar pattern, the invaders crossing the Channel or the North Sea to land on the south or east coast, then moved westward, pressing the inhabitants slowly back into the Welsh mountains. Here the invaders were invariably held up and the two counties of Herefordshire and Shropshire became the 'Western Frontier of England'.

Advance outposts against the Welsh

While Worcestershire might have been regarded as the main stop-line against the Welsh making retaliatory raids from their mountains down into the fertile and, to them, enemy occupied territory, it was the counties of Herefordshire and Shropshire which provided the advanced line of outposts.

The military geography of Herefordshire, as far as hillforts, Roman camps, Norman and medieval castles are concerned, can be divided into two parts. The most important is the county's far western boundary where it impinges on the foothills of the Welsh mountains, and where the first shock of the countless raids was taken. The other is the far eastern boundary where for some miles the main stop-line ran along the Malvern Hills, and lies within Herefordshire. Between these two lines lies a flatish area twenty-five miles wide, not exactly a no man's land, but devoid of any physical features that might have been used for defensive works.

Hillforts

The Malvern Hills form an eight-mile-long, narrow, steep, and acute ridge, never more than a mile and usually less than half-a-mile wide, running north and south to the west of Great Malvern and Malvern Wells. The most northerly two miles of this ridge lie within Worcestershire and are outside this chapter, but a brief digression across the county boundary must be made to the Worcestershire Beacon, almost 1,400 feet high. From this eminence can be seen three cathedrals (Gloucester, Hereford and Worcester), six great abbeys (including Evesham, Pershore, and Tewkesbury), and, most important for the military historian, six great battlefields of English history: Edgehill, Evesham, Mortimer's Cross, Shrewsbury, Tewkesbury, and Worcester. Along the top of this northern section of the hills, especially around the summit, can be seen the remnants of fortifications. Unfortunately it needs a fit and agile person to visit the higher sites. The nearest road, although only a quarter of a mile away, is 800 feet below and the gradient is steep.

The more southerly three-quarters of the ridge lie within or on the Herefordshire boundary, and the succession of hilltops provides many examples of hillforts. Perseverance Hill, Pinnacle Hill, Herefordshire Beacon, Hangman's Hill, Midsummer Hill, Ragged Stone Hill (900 feet high) all show traces of works.

Immediately west of Little Malvern – on the eastern side of the main ridge – a road from Ledbury to Upton-on-Severn passes through a cutting in the great ridge, Wynds Point. Here is a very old inn, called the 'British Camp Hotel'. Parts of the building date back to the fifteenth century and it is almost certain that a much older building, also probably an inn, stood in this isolated pass through the Malvern Hills. It is quite certain that the Scottish army of Charles II used this pass, and doubtless the inn, on its way to the Battle of Worcester in 1651.

Overleaf Slopes of the Malvern Hills from Worcestershire Beacon.

Hillfort at Coxall Knoll, Herefordshire.

Immediately south of the inn and on the opposite side of the road a steep path leads up to the Herefordshire Beacon, 1,100 feet high. On the summit and around several of the sides will be found one of the finest earthworks in Great Britain. It was built about 200 BC and altered before the Roman Conquest 300 years later. The camp is a mile and three quarters in circumference, enclosing forty-five acres. The great entrenchments, still in remarkable preservation, are often eight feet deep, and in places are thirty feet across. The camp citadel at the top is defended by a stone wall and a deep 'last ditch'. It must have been virtually impregnable. It was unquestionably a permanent fort, built to protect the pass below it, and was not a place for emergency defence. It is believed that Caractacus, one of the last English chieftains to resist the Romans, held out in this camp for a long time.

Herefordshire Beacon

The most striking physical feature of the Herefordshire Beacon is, on its western face, the remarkably steep slope of the hill. Although not sheer, the gradient must be at least 60° to the horizontal, say 1 in 2. An able-bodied young man, in climbing gear and unencumbered with arms, shields etc., even today could only climb it by using both hands and feet. An attacker, presumably having to face arrows, or more likely boulders thrown from above, must have been completely out of breath and for a few minutes quite useless, on reaching the main entrenchment.

Herefordshire Beacon is easier to reach than the Worcestershire Beacon. The car park is often full in the summer, and the footpaths are not too difficult or steep.

Farther south, Midsummer Hill is worth a visit, and its footpath from near Hollybush on the Ledbury-Tewkesbury road is by no means difficult although rather lengthy. This hill has innumerable entrenchments on every side of the summit. Ragged Stone Hill, 500 yards south of Hollybush, has a cart track, possible for a car with careful driving, a good footpath up to the summit and is very similar to the tops of other hills along the entire Malvern range, except that there are no signs of entrenchments. From a tactical point of view it seems certain that some must have existed in the past. Together with those on Midsummer Hill they would have been a formidable protection to the road passing between and below them. If Ragged Stone Hill had not been fortified and held, an enemy could have occupied it and become a serious menace to the pass below. Possibly the vestiges of barely discernible works may be the remains of entrenchments, but if they are, why have they so disintegrated when their counterparts on the other hill-tops in the same ridge stand out so clearly?

The line of hillforts along the Malvern Hills does not, of course, end at its northern end. It continues northward for six miles on lower but tactically still good positions and passes into Worcestershire.

The Western Frontier of England

The far western boundary of Herefordshire was the more important of the two defence lines of the Western Frontier of England. Here the retiring Britons, driven westward from the fertile lands of the western counties by the invaders from the Continent passed into the natural strongholds of the country in front of them, the Welsh mountains. These invaders were followed in their turn by the Romans and the Saxons and often the defeated refugee troops mingled with the existing native tribesmen of the mountains. A strong sense of defeat and injustice animated these mountain dwellers. Frequent retaliatory raids against the invaders who had pressed them into these inhospitable regions were launched, and hillforts to hold these incursions were built along the foothills out in front of the main range.

The hillfort of Croft Ambrey near Aymestrey is well worth a visit but is difficult to reach. It lies almost a mile to the north of Croft Castle, which is two miles north-east of Mortimer's Cross, but involves a rough two-mile walk through woods and up a ridge. Several others, widely spread, are of interest. Combe, on the B4362 Presteigne-Shobden road, has not only a hillfort on Wapley Hill, half-a-mile to the south of the road, approached partway by a minor road leading to Combe Wood, and then a climb of 300 feet. In addition, on the opposite side of the main road, is 'Castle Mound' on the banks of the River Lugg and covering the only bridge for two miles in either direction. Clearly it is an important tactical position but the mound seems much younger than the earliest and may well be Roman or even probably Norman. Coxall Knoll, north-west from Brampton Bryan on the A4113, Knighton-Ludlow road, has an extensive fort which can be reached easily by car to within 300 yards. Burfa Camp, although technically 200 yards beyond the Herefordshire county border, should be visited. It is half-a-mile north-west of Knill on the B4362, New Radnor–Presteigne road, and is but 200 yards from the roadside, up a fairly steep climb. To the south of the little village of Knill and opposite Knill Court is Rushock Hill. Along the northern crest of this 1,200 foot-high mountain, if it may be so called, is a mile-and-a-half stretch of Offa's Dyke. The usual climb up from the road is steep and hard-going but the walk is considerably easier if you take a cart track running south-west from the ford over the Hindwell Brook just east of Knill Court. Aconbury Hill, four miles south of Hereford City has an extensive hillfort and is easily reached from

Overleaf Herefordshire Beacon, one of the finest earthworks in Great Britain. Built *c.* 200 BC and improved three hundred years later by the Romans. Note the three lines of trenches and the extreme difficulties for any attacker.

the main Hereford-Monmouth road, while Dinedor Camp, north of Dinedor Cross, is just off to the left of the Hereford-Little Dewchurch road and only two miles south of Hereford. One particularly fine example is Sutton Walls, about four miles north of Hereford. An oblong camp, half a mile long from east to west, and two hundred yards from north to south, is in excellent condition. There are traces of foundations of prehistoric huts, and within it a considerable quantity of Roman debris, pottery, iron instruments, etc., has been found. The camp stands a few hundred yards to the north of the hamlet of Sutton St Michael. It commands two bridges over the River Lugg which was originally crossed here by fords. Although on a slight eminence it is easy to reach on foot, and a car can be driven very close.

These are but a few examples of the many fortified hilltops, mostly prehistoric but sometimes Roman, in Herefordshire. All are marked on the map by the conventional sign for an earthwork. They are more or less difficult of access, but all are rewarding to the active historian-traveller. Overshadowing them all is the great Offa's Duke.

Offa's Dyke

This gigantic earthwork was built about AD 780 by King Offa, the great king of Mercia. He intended it for two purposes. First, political as a boundary line for all men to see and in particular to show the Welsh exactly where their country ended and his began. Second, military, as a defensive ditch intended to keep raiders out. It ran from Prestatyn on the Dee estuary in the north and passed southward through the counties of Flintshire, Denbighshire, Shropshire, Montgomeryshire, Radnorshire, Herefordshire and finally through Gloucestershire, where it joined the River Wye, altogether about 120 miles. From Welshpool in Montgomeryshire southward through Shropshire to near Presteigne in Radnorshire the great Dyke is largely continuous but thence and along most of its line through Herefordshire a good deal of it has disappeared. The best examples of it lie to the immediate east of the River Arrow, between Shawl and Lyonshall Wood, a mile and a half east of Kington. As has already been described there is a stretch near Knill. It seems probable that the many gaps in its construction were left because in these areas it ran through dense woods, which in the Saxon era were considered to be impassable. In Shropshire, Offa's Dyke is seen in all its glory.

The Romans

There are considerable Roman military remains in Herefordshire. As was seen in the chapter on Worcestershire the Romans did not reach Herefordshire until four years after they had landed at Deal in AD 43. Here they came up against the line of hillforts built by the earlier prehistoric invaders, who had built them to resist the Welsh raiders. But these forts now faced the wrong way and their occupiers had to re-orientate them to face east instead of west. They were by no means unsuccessful in resisting the Romans, and it took these new invaders thirty years before all the forts were reduced and they could advance into Wales in AD 78.

During this delay the Romans occupied themselves in Herefordshire by laying out settlements which were sometimes temporary military encampments as well as townships. Kentchester, five miles westward of Hereford on the Brecon road was, as its name implies, an important garrison. Its remains lie just to the north of the hamlet of Bunshill and south of the present village of Kentchester. They appear to have been headquarters of the Roman army of occupation in the Herefordshire area. The camp makes an easy and fairly interesting walk from Banshill. A mile-and-a-half along the Roman road from Kentchester towards Brecon, the road passes over Offa's Dyke.

The village of Leintwardine, on the A4113 Ludlow-Knighton road must not be missed. It is on the site of a small Roman station, Bravonium, and has much to show. The settlement is enclosed by rectangular earthworks, clearly seen on its western side and at the north-west angle. They may be faintly traced elsewhere although the modern village growth has damaged and sometimes obliterated them. The east part of Leintwardine church is built exactly on the Roman bank, and consequently there is a striking difference in floor levels within the church. The Roman road through the settlement is today the High Street.

During the thirty years when the Roman armies were pressing the defending Britons back into Wales, the settlement of the fertile valley of Herefordshire went on apace. There are many small Roman village settlements, many villas, many well built and well laid out roads, and it is clear that this was a thickly populated colony. After a while Roman soldiers were well received and some married Herefordshire women. But this peaceful colonization was largely civilian and does not concern us in this book.

The site of the Roman garrison town of Kentchester. The variation in this crop of barley reveals the position of underground masonry courses.

Head of an Iron Age axe found on the site of Kentchester in 1944.

The dark ages

The next era in Herefordshire's history, the Dark Ages, from AD 415 when the Romans withdrew from the British Isles until the Norman invasion of 1066, is rather meagre in military history. For 150 years after AD 415 a dark peace descended upon most of England, and little is known about these years nor is it probable that there is much to know. But about AD 600 the Saxon invasion moved slowly across England, overwhelming most of the Roman-British settlements in slaughter and desolation. Kentchester was destroyed as was Viroconium. This last, an important Roman settlement, lay two miles to the east of Ross-on-Wye, near the village of Weston-under-Penyard but it had no military connections.

The Norman Invasion of 1066 did not make much impact on Herefordshire for some years. But in 1086 the Domesday Book was compiled and from it William the Conqueror saw the large number of English/Saxon landowners along the Welsh border. They were powerful men locally, and obviously anti-Norman. William saw what a potential danger they were should they combine against him, or, more dangerous still, join forces with the Welsh, only a few miles away. There was a good deal of Welsh blood in the people along the border, and it would have needed little to unite them against the hated and efficient foreigners.

William's nominees

William acted reasonably albeit harshly, and evicted many of these powerful families, replacing them in their great houses with his own Norman nominees, of whose loyalty he was in no doubt, and on whom he could rely to fight against Welsh raids. He encouraged them to fortify their new homes, to build keeps, and moats, and to turn them into isolated fortified posts. He achieved two goals by doing this: he bound his subordinates to him more closely through their gratitude, and secured his western frontier at someone else's expense.

A sketch map showing these now considerable military fortifications appearing in the two outpost counties of Herefordshire and Shropshire, when superimposed on a similar map showing the prehistoric and Roman defence works in the same area, makes a striking picture of the western frontier. Its strategic importance is clearly evident. It is a broad band, thirty-five miles wide, and sixty miles long. It was in its 2,000 years of history the scene of numberless raids, defensive actions and fracas. A map of fortified manors and castles in Herefordshire in about AD 1300 shows that for every two manors east of the Wye and the Lugg (which roughly bisect the county there are nearly double that number to the west of the rivers, and up against the western border.

It is impossible to describe all of these fortified manors. Many have disappeared, but those that survive, usually in ruins, are indeed worthy of a visit.

Castle ruins

Goodrich Castle is the best of them all. Every feature of a great Norman castle can be seen, and its entirety seen at a glance. The keep especially is of absorbing interest, and seems to be impregnable. The Clare family owned it, and it was the last castle in Herefordshire to hold out for King Charles I. After his execution Cromwell ordered it to be unroofed and left to decay. It lies midway between Ross and Monmouth, and is half a mile north of the village of Goodrich. A walk of 500 yards from the Goodrich–Pencraig road is unavoidable.

Wigmore Castle, on the A4110 Leominster–Knighton road still has portions of its original building. It was the great stronghold of the Mortimers, one of the most powerful families in England in Norman and early medieval eras. Although not so belligerent or aggressive as the Percys in Northumberland the Mortimers were quite as influential politically, socially and as leadership. More will be heard of the Mortimer family in the account of the battle of Mortimer's Cross in the Wars of the Roses.

The castle ruins are half-a-mile north-west of the village of Wigmore, and can be reached by car along a cart-track off to the left on leaving the village. Regrettably the castle has been badly neglected and is thickly overgrown with bushes and undergrowth, which make appreciation of the different parts of the castle and enjoyment of their interest difficult. It was originally built before 1066 – and much altered and added to in the twelfth, thirteenth and fourteenth centuries. Its decay and general disintegration however seem to have been somehow arrested, and an engraving of 1732 shows the castle very much as it is today. In view of the importance

Opposite Snodhill Castle, Peterchurch, Herefordshire. The keep seen from the south.

Previous pages Goodrich Castle, near Ross-on-Wye, has every feature of a Norman castle and its symmetrical plan is seen clearly from the air. The bastions grow out of the natural rock. It was the last castle in Herefordshire to hold out for Charles I. Cromwell ordered the castle to be unroofed and left to decay.

of its owners for many centuries, it should be visited.

The remains of Ewyas Harold Castle are close to the Welsh border midway between Hereford and Abergavenny on the A465. They lie close to the second-class road, Ewyas Harold–Newton, and bear the engaging name of Castle Tump. Today they are no more than a gigantic heap of turf-covered rubble, but are of interest because of their great antiquity – built in the reign of Edward the Confessor – and also because of their proximinity to the frontier four miles away and thus directly in the line of Welsh raiding parties.

Yet another village with forts is even closer, Walterstone, only half a mile from the frontier. It is of interest because there is a prehistoric fort half a mile to the east of the church, overlooking the River Monnaw, and only 200 yards' walk from Grove Farm. On the west, close to the church, are the remains of Walterstone Castle. Little is to be seen, but the ditch surrounding the keep is still thirty feet deep.

Richard's Castle is a village partly in Herefordshire and partly in Shropshire, on the B4361 Leominster-Orleton-Ludford road. Turn left in the village and a mile farther on the parish church is seen to the left just as the road turns sharply to the right. Two hundred yards to the west is the castle. It is mentioned in Domesday Book and thus was built before 1086, and is possibly pre-1066. It was another of several great strongholds owned and held by the Mortimers. Its central motte (not to be confused with 'moat'), the raised earth mound, is sixty-five yards in diameter at its base, its summit being sixty feet above its protective ditch. One of the walls on the north side of the bailey, the open space in the centre of all medieval castles, is still twelve feet high. It is an enormous edifice and worth visiting as it is so easily found, and approached.

Castles in occupation today

All the foregoing castles or manor houses are in ruins and quite uninhabitable. But the following are still lived in and can be visited during the summer. Croft Castle, on the B4362 Tenbury Wells-Mortimer's Cross road, is magnificent. It has been lived in by the Croft family for over 900 years, and is mentioned in Domesday Book. The four main outer walls, and their round corner towers survive, although restored. On the Croft Castle estate and about a mile to the north of the castle is Croft Ambrey – a spectacular Iron Age hillfort, used as a military centre and defensive post from 300 BC until AD 50.

Hellen's at Much Marcle on the A499 Ledbury-Ross road is of interest. Lived in since 1292 it is the home of the Pennington-Mellor-Munthe family. In the great hall is the stone table at which the Black Prince dined, and upstairs is the bedroom prepared for Queen Mary I – 'Bloody Mary' – in 1554.

Kentchurch Court, to the east of the village which is two miles south-east of Pontrilas on the Abergavenny-Hereford road, is another fortified border manor house. The gateway and original fourteenth-century house survive. Lastly Pembridge Castle, four miles north of Monmouth and a mile north-west of Welsh Newton off the A466, is still occupied and dates from about 1250.

Other border castles, now in ruins, and not of great interest are Eardisley, Bollitree, Kinnersley and Huntington.

Peace comes to the Welsh border

The ever-present threat of aggression, raids and sorties from the Welsh hills kept Herefordshire in a state of readiness from the time of Domesday Book (1086) until 1282. Admittedly the danger gradually decreased in these 200 years, but the castles and fortified manors were always in the front defensive line, their owners always had their ear to the ground and vigilance, although decreasing, had to be maintained.

In 1282 Edward I finally subdued Wales, proclaiming his infant son, born in Caernarvon Castle in 1284, as Prince of Wales. Peace did not come overnight, but after the Prince's proclamation the Welsh felt themselves now recognized by and acceptable to the English, and the turbulence on the Western Frontier of England slowly died away. For almost 200 years Herefordshire faded out of the history of England.

Opposite Pembridge Castle, four miles north of Monmouth, dates from 1250.

The Wars of the Roses

But in 1461 the county came back into the limelight very largely because of the Wars of the Roses (and the existence of the Mortimer family). The confused course of the Wars of the Roses was principally bedevilled by the weakness, sometimes madness, of King Henry VI, the considerable claim of Richard, Duke of York to the throne, the masterful personality of Richard Neville, Earl of Warwick, and lastly the marriages of the Warwick family (Yorkists), with that of the Somersets (Lancastrians).

The first two battles of the Wars of the Roses, the First St Albans and Bloreheath, were won by the Yorkists. The next, a minor skirmish at Ludlow was gained by the Lancastrians, where the Yorkists panicked and ran. York withdrew to Ireland, while most of the Yorkist knights fled to France, including young Prince Edward, Earl of March, the eldest son of the Duke of York. This boy was now aged eighteen.

He was the grandson of Anne Mortimer. There were two other Mortimers in the maternal genealogical tree before Anne whose grandfather had been Lionel, Duke of Clarence, second son of Edward III. On the other side of young Edward's family his paternal grandfather was the son of Edmund, Duke of York, fourth son of Edward III. Young Prince Edward, and his father before him, Richard, Duke of York (killed at Wakefield), had undoubted claims to the throne of England, and it is difficult to avoid sympathy for them in their frustration, and also to disagree that the Yorkist claim to the crown was at least as good as that of the Lancastrians. But they had no hope whatever of establishing their claim, just as the four generations before them had no hope of throwing the three Lancastrian monarchs, Henry IV, V and VI, off the throne except by force of arms and civil war.

The Battle of Mortimer's Cross.

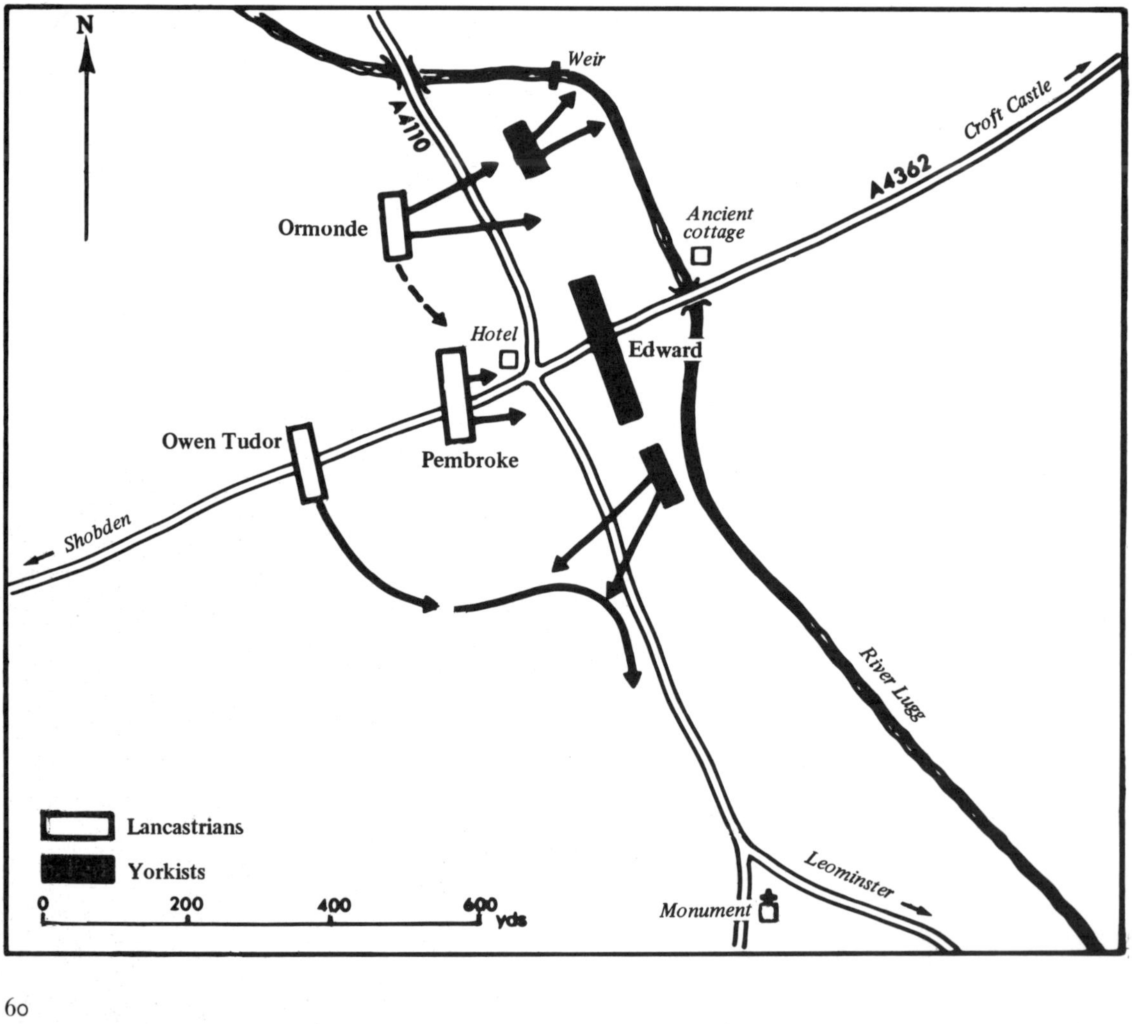

BATTLE OF MORTIMER'S CROSS

In the year following the Ludlow defeat the Duke of York returned from Ireland to meet his subordinate knights back from France. They were all determined to take up their cause again. They at once collected an army to march north and meet the royal army in the Midlands. They detached young Edward of March to go down into the West Country and Wales, there to recruit an army to move up to support York.

Both the Duke of York and his son, young Edward, were descendants of the Mortimer family, and the Yorkist party knew full well that the family in Herefordshire was perhaps the most influential and powerful family in the West country. What more likely than a rush of recruits to join the standard of the young Prince?

Not only the family of Mortimer but many families from all walks of life in Herefordshire believed that this attractive boy, well set-up and old for his years, was the rightful heir to the throne and that if York succeeded in his campaign Edward must eventually be their king. Not only loyalty to the Mortimer family but concern for their own future drove many to young Edward's side. The optimism regarding his mission to raise a supporting army was justified, and he very quickly collected several hundred good quality yeoman farmers from the Welsh borders, good horsemen and well mounted. Among them were a few townsmen from Ludlow, Leominster and Presteigne, but these were poorly armed and had little training, although they possessed great morale.

At the end of January Edward had collected his very sketchy army around Hereford. To escape the numerically superior Lancastrian forces moving towards Worcester from the west and trying to come between him and London, he moved away to the north for seventeen miles and reached a crossroads deep in the Herefordshire countryside, Mortimer's Cross. Here the River Lugg flowing south to join the Wye, after passing through a steep-sided defile, emerges on to flatter ground. At the crossroads are a few cottages, an hotel and, about 300 yards away, a bridge over the river. Edward placed his army between the road up from

Mortimer's Cross today. The Lancastrian line ran along the road facing to the left. The Earl of Ormonde's attack crossed about where the road curves out of sight to the left.

Hereford, the river with its bridge and the crossroads all facing west, and waited. The ground is flat, low-lying, and in January very muddy.

Edward's poor position

Tactically Edward's position was poor. Only two hundred yards behind, and along his entire line ran the River Lugg, about three feet deep, and with banks five feet high on average. A severe reverse anywhere along the line would push his troops into the river behind them which must have created a great obstacle to headlong retreat, giving the pursuing attackers an opportunity to do great damage. Immediately in front of his centre but over the crossroads was a considerable hill 400 feet high, rising to almost 700 feet. Occupation of this hill would give the attacking Lancastrians a dominating position overlooking the entire field.

The position of the defenders at Mortimer's Cross is very like that taken up by the defending Lancastrians at Hexham in 1464. There Henry VI had his back to the river, Devil's Water, very similar in dimensions to the Lugg. In front of him stood the hill, Dipton Wood. The Yorkists charged down the hill against the Lancastrians who were drawn up with their backs to the river. The impetus of the downhill run carried the Yorkists through the defending lines and up to the river, where those Lancastrians who had escaped the charge found themselves gravely hindered in their headlong retreat by the river and its steep and difficult banks.

At Mortimer's Cross, Edward should have occupied the hill beyond the crossroads, up which the Lancastrians would have been forced to climb. A strong detachment should have been sent down the Shopden road to the west to delay the Lancastrian advance, and could indeed have occupied an excellent delaying position astride the road, at Mortimer's Rock. The only reason for not seeing this excellent tactical position, and for occupying the bad position, is that infantry tactics, use of ground, and an eye for the terrain were not known or practised in the fifteenth century. Head-on collisions were the only infantry tactics. Nevertheless, Edward won the battle of Mortimer's Cross, despite his badly-sited defensive position, a victory that says little for the military skill, and even less for the morale, of the Lancastrians.

Collapse of the Lancastrians

On 2 February at daybreak, a Lancastrian force came up the road from the west through Shopden three miles to the south-west under the command of the Earl of Pembroke. A strong attack under the Earl of Ormonde against Edward's right group around the weir 300 yards north of the crossroads succeeded in pushing this group back to the river and there it disintegrated. Many Yorkists were killed and the survivors waded across the river, here about five feet deep. At the same time the middle Lancastrian brigade, under Pembroke himself, attacked the Yorkist centre under Edward's personal command at and to the south of the crossroads but was repulsed with very heavy losses. Ormonde's successful left wing group now returned to the field to reinforce Pembroke in the centre only to find him defeated. Ormonde's men then sat down just west of the crossroads and awaited events.

The last uncommitted Lancastrian group on the right flank under Owen Tudor now tried to move round the Yorkists' left flank midway between New House Farm and Mortimer's Cross. But Edward's left group, so far without a fight, advanced on the exposed left flank of this Lancastrian attempt at an outflanking manoeuvre, and cut it in two. The whole attacking Lancastrian army now collapsed, most of them retreating south-east down the present A4110 road to Leominster. Owen Tudor, the commander of this Lancastrian right wing, was captured. Edward, moving forward, had difficulty in restraining his men from killing the wounded.

Next day Edward marched down into Hereford with his captive, Owen Tudor, whom he hanged publicly in the market-place. Owen Tudor was the grandfather of Henry Tudor, who as Henry VII and the victor at Bosworth in 1485 was England's first Tudor monarch, father of Henry VIII and grandfather of Queen Elizabeth I.

Edward then turned for London, and by forced marches reached the capital a few days later, where he declared himself King Edward IV, his father the Duke of York having been killed at the Battle of Wakefield five weeks earlier.

This quite unimportant little battle of the Wars of the Roses has two noteworthy features. It gave Edward experience in commanding in battle an independent force and thus paved the way for his three other great successes. He was to rule England for twelve years, and led the Yorkists to victory at Mortimer's Cross, Towton Moor, Barnet, and Tewkesbury. He was England's greatest soldier-king and it is sad that his moral character in middle and later life fell far short of his other great qualities.

Memorial erected in 1779 to the battle of Mortimer's Cross. It is a mile and a half from the crossroads, where the B.4360 branches off.

This Pedestal is erected to perpetuate the Memory
of an obstinate, bloody and decisive battle, fought near
this Spot in the civil War between the ambitious Houses
of York and Lancaster, on the 2d Day of February 1460
between the Forces of Edward Mortimer Earl of
March (afterwards Edward the Fourth) on the Side of
York and those of Henry the Six, on the Side of
Lancaster.
The Kings Troops were commanded by Jasper Earl
of Pembroke, Edward commanded his own in Person, and
was victorious. The Slaughter was great on both Sides
four Thousand being left dead on the Field, and many
Welsh Persons of the first distinction were taken Prisoners
among whom was Owen Tudor (Great Grandfather to
Henry the Eighth, and a Descendant of the illustrious
Cadwallader) who was afterwards beheaded at Hereford
This was the decisive Battle which fixed Edward the
Fourth on the Throne of England who was proclaimed
King in London on the fifth of March following.
Erected by Subscription
in the Year 1799

Secondly Mortimer's Cross is a battlefield that is easily found, comfortably examined, and can be seen in its entirety from the excellent viewpoint of the bridge 200 yards to the east of the crossroads.

The battlefield in its entirety
Immediately over the bridge on slightly rising ground, and only 150 yards from the field where most of the fighting took place an occupied cottage stands today. The lowermost southerly two rooms are the original building put up in 1450. The upper window in 1461 would have provided a ringside seat for the action. To the north of the little road leading from Mortimer's Cross to the bridge are the meadows wherein the Earl of Ormonde pushed Edward's right wing back into the river. Astride this little road and to its south Pembroke's central group attacked Edward and was repulsed. About 300 yards to the south of the crossroads and standing beside the road was, in 1461, a giant oak, known for many years as Battle Oak. Regrettably it was blown down recently and although still shown on the large-scale Ordnance Survey maps, has now disappeared. About a mile and a quarter south from Mortimer's Cross and on the B4360 is a fork-road; in the angle between the two arms, is the battle memorial erected in 1779. Why it was erected here, at least half a mile from the last scene of the battle (Edward's left flank advance to cut in half the Lancastrian right) is not clear. Very close to the crossroads, the centre of the battlefield where there is plenty of room seems to be the obvious choice. Perhaps one day it will be moved to a more historically accurate site.

Hereford City

The city of Hereford, a charming, quiet, west country county town with, in 1973, 40,000 inhabitants, has much history. About AD 70 the Romans arrived to guard the crossing of the River Wye. After thirty years they moved on to found Kentchester, doubtless leaving a considerable garrison behind to guard the crossing. There are no signs or records of any earthworks or fortifications, but investigations suggest that Church Street formed the central street through the settlement, whose northern limit was out beyond the present East Street and Broad Street.

Hereford Cathedral. The first cathedral was built by Offa, and Hereford thus became one of the earliest dioceses in England.

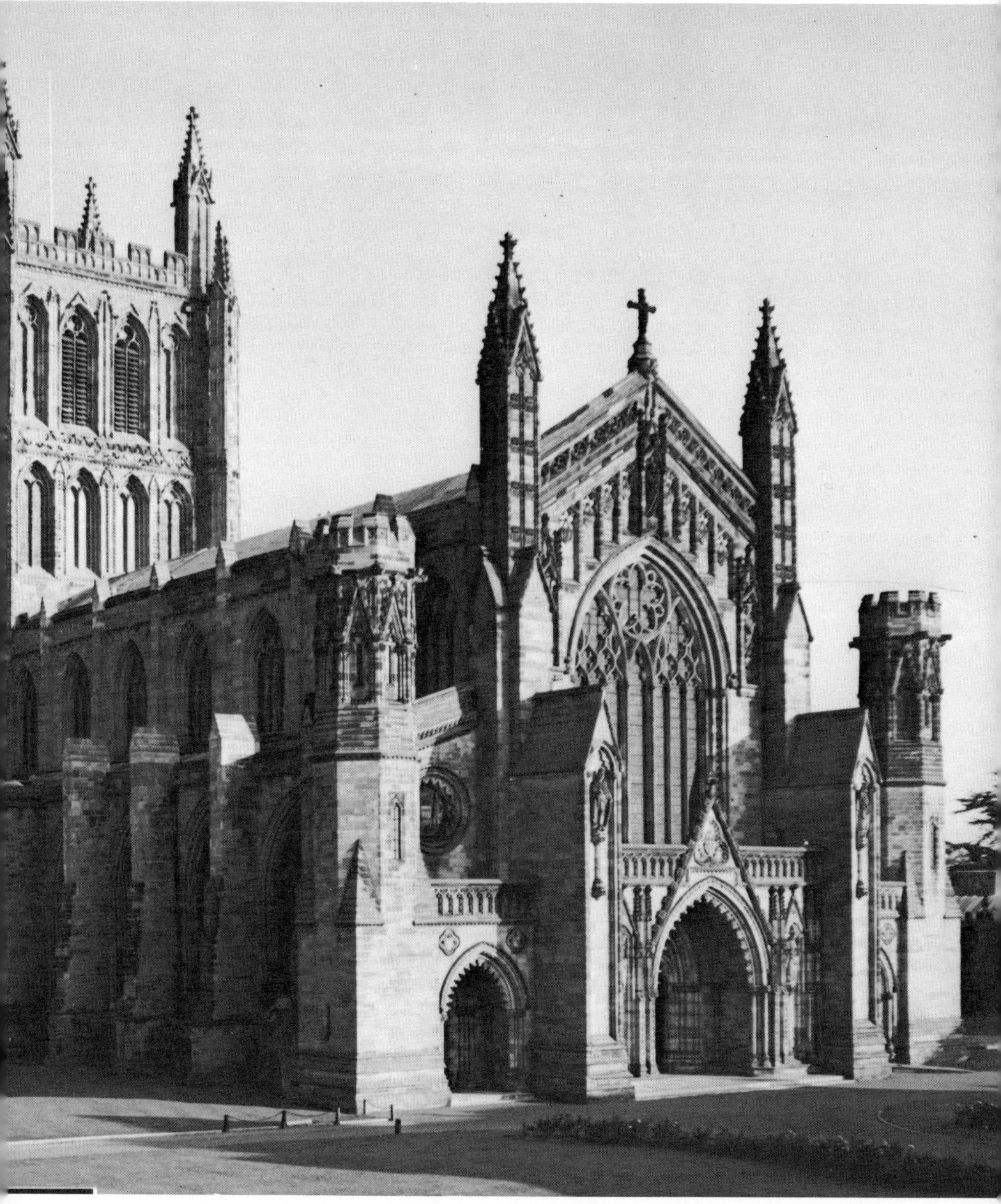

The town became an important base for the Saxons in their campaigns against the Welsh and it grew rapidly in the eighth century. A cathedral was built by Offa and a diocese formed around it, Hereford thus becoming one of the earliest of English dioceses.

After the death of Offa in 796 Hereford dwindled in importance and little is known of its history for the next 250 years beyond the fact that in 1055 the Welsh made a great attack on it. They defeated a mixed force of English and Saxons, together with some Norman mercenary soldiers near the present-day suburb of Holmer, probably on what is now the racecourse, and afterwards burnt the town and cathedral. The following year the Welsh were yet again pushed back into their own country, and Hereford was rebuilt by Harold Godwin, of Hastings fame. The new defences consisted of a ditch and rampart; a small section of this rampart, now 900 years old, can still be seen in Victoria Street. On Castle Green in the south-east corner of the city, stood the castle. This is now a park with no remains of the original building left. The castle and nearly the whole length of the walls were standing and in excellent condition as late as about 1650. The castle had an almost square outer wall, the most southerly side of which faced on to the river Wye. In the centre on a considerable, and artificial, mound stood the inner bailey, in the centre of which was the keep, a six-sided building topped with massive castellations.

The decline of the Welsh raiding menace in 1282 was followed by the decline of the military usefulness, or even need, of the Norman castles and fortified manors. Herefordshire was to enjoy an era of peace for 363 years, and with one exception there are no military events to be chronicled through this period. But both the city of Hereford and the county of Hereford came briefly back into English history in the Civil War.

In April 1645 the town of Ledbury was held for the Parliamentarians with a thousand men. Prince Rupert, Charles I's nephew, riding from Hereford City up to Shrewsbury decided to turn aside and attack Ledbury with his cavalry and infantry. Charging down the long wide High Street he drove the Parliamentarians before him, dispersing them finally near the Church of St Michael and All Angels. Shortly after this unimportant little skirm-

Castle Green, Hereford. The monument to the right marks the site of the original castle built 900 years ago.

ish, some bullets were prised out of the west door of the church and are preserved in a glass case in St Katherine's Chapel. St Katherine's was an almshouse dating back to the thirteenth century but the present buildings were erected on the original site in 1822. In the little battle Major Backhouse, a Parliamentarian, was mortally wounded, and carried into a house near by where he died. His sword was hidden in the roof of this house where it remained long forgotten for nearly 250 years. In 1888 it was discovered deep in grime and dust under the rafters. Cleaned, it was added to the case holding the bullets from the church door, and all now rest in St Katherine's Chapel.

The siege

Three months later the city of Hereford itself was besieged. Primarily it was Royalist in sympathy, being close to Wales whence King Charles derived much of his support. On the outbreak of war its defences were strengthened and a larger garrison of troops was quartered in the castle. This was a wise proceeding because a large force of Parliamentarian-sympathizing Scotsmen under the Earl of Leven arrived under its walls, demanding surrender. This often foolish step had its usual result; the surrender was refused, strengthening the determination to resist and the people of the city took up arms to reinforce the garrison. A spirited siege and defence ensued, lasting nearly five weeks. Hearing of the approach of King Charles with a relieving force the Scots withdrew.

The Wye Bridge, Hereford. Defenders in the siege of Hereford during the Civil War had to destroy the arch at right of picture to hold the Parliamentarians.

At times the defenders had been hard put to it to hold the town bridge over the Wye and eventually they were compelled to break down one of its arches. After the war the bridge was repaired and the new arch, clearly seen at the northern end of the bridge is a permanent memorial to the siege.

The raising of this siege of Hereford in the Civil War of 1645 was almost the last event of any military importance that either the city of Hereford or the county was to witness on its own soil. But not quite. Almost 300 years after the siege, Hereford again tasted violence and actual warfare. In July 1942 a German air-raid searching for the munition factory dropped bombs killing several people.

HEREFORDSHIRE'S REGIMENTS

Although no further military operations occurred in the county, Herefordshire remained in the military picture. After the disbandment of Cromwell's New Model Army in 1661 Charles II and his government realized the necessity of having some permanent standing force to defend the country against aggression from overseas and to preserve the peace at home. Consequently Regular Regiments, known by their number only, were raised through the next forty-five years. In 1702, forty-one years after the disbandment of Cromwell's regiments, the 36th Regiment of Foot was born.

Regimental badge of the Herefordshire Light Infantry before amalgamation with the Worcester Regiment in 1881.

The history of The Herefordshire Regiment, as the 36th was to become, is, it is believed, unique. There have been two Herefordshire Regiments, neither connected with the other.

The 36th Foot

The first, the 36th Foot, the Regular regiment, was raised in 1702. In 1782 it was redesignated The 36th (Herefordshire) Regiment. It served with distinction in India and then in the Peninsular War. After the latter campaign it had been awarded the Regimental motto of 'Firm'. It retained its Herefordshire identity until 1881 when, in the Cardwell reforms of the infantry that year, it lost its title and number, to become the 2nd Battalion of the Worcestershire Regiment.

The battalion was stationed in Aldershot in August 1914 and took part, in the 2nd Division, in the battles of Mons, Le Cateau and the Great Retreat.

In October 1914 it carried out the famous charge of the Worcesters at Gheluvelt in the 1st Battle of Ypres in 1914. This charge has been described in some detail in the chapter on Worcestershire.

In the great reduction of the infantry in 1953 the Worcesters, who had already lost their 3rd and 4th Battalions in 1922, suffered yet another disbandment; this time it was the 2nd Battalion, the old 36th Herefordshire Regiment, the Regiment that brought the Worcesters their present motto, 'Firm', and it passed out of military history – perhaps only temporarily?

C Company (Herefordshire) Light Infantry Volunteers

The other Herefordshire Regiment was a Territorial battalion. Like four others it came from counties that had no Regular Regiment. The Hertfords, the Cambridgeshires, the Huntingdons, and the Monmouths were all independent and had no parent or elder brother. This territorial Hereford battalion originated from eleven Rifle Volunteer Corps which had been raised in 1860, during the revival of patriotism that occurred after the Crimean War and the Indian Mutiny. In 1880 they were all amalgamated into a unit now to be designated the 1st Herefordshire Rifle Volunteer Corps. In 1908 in the Haldane reforms the unit was again given a new name, the 1st Herefordshire Regiment and affiliated to the King's Shropshire Light Infantry. In 1947 the words 'Light Infantry' were restored to its title in place of 'Regiment'. It still exists as 'C' Company (Herefordshire) in The Light Infantry Volunteers, a battalion composed of similar companies from other disbanded, or vastly reduced, Territorial battalions in the West Midlands.

About 10 May 1940 and before the final evacuation from Dunkirk it became evident that Great Britain's army in France was virtually defeated and was about to be thrown into the sea. Only the Navy and the RAF stood between us and Germany, with no British army.

On 14 May the Secretary of State for War, Anthony Eden, broadcast to the nation calling for all able-bodied men over seventeen and under sixty-five to volunteer at once as spare-time soldiers to defend the country. Mr Eden said, 'Since the war started the government has received countless enquiries from men of all ages who wish to do something active in the defence of their country. Now is your chance. You will not be paid. You will, of course, receive arms and uniforms as they become available.'

Cigarette card of 1908 showing the standard and (Boer War) uniform of the 1st Herefordshire Regiment who were to be affiliated with the King's Shropshire Light Infantry in that year.

In Herefordshire in at least one instance Mr Eden's call to raise the Home Guard had been anticipated. In March, two months before the disaster to the French Army in France and then the retreat to Dunkirk, and before Mr Eden's broadcast, a certain Lady Helena Gleichen living in her ancestral home at Much Marcle, between Ledbury and Ross, had felt great concern regarding the possibility of German parachute troops landing in the thinly-populated areas of Herefordshire and the Welsh border. She therefore organized her domestic staff and tenantry, to the number of eighty, into teams of watchmen whom she stationed daily on the high ground near her home at Much Marcle. Known as the Much Marcle Watchers, each morning and evening one party went 'on watch', each man wearing a luminous arm band, stencilled 'MMW'. She asked the local battalion of the KSLI to lend her eighty rifles, and ammunition and two machine-guns '. . . if you can spare them'. The CO of the KSLI had to call up his greatest powers of argument and dominance, to meet the almost unanswerable case of this most masterful lady. Nevertheless, two months before the Home Guard was formed here was the first illegitimate unit, complete with watchers, arm-bands, organization, command, and no arms.

Herefordshire raised six battalions of the Home Guard. Four were based on Leominster, Bromyard, Ross, and Harewood End, the latter being a tiny little village in the heart of an intensely rural area, about five miles north-west of Ross. The other two were raised in or around Hereford City. These six battalions, with the exception of one in the city, were all trained as infantry soldiers, to manoeuvre across country, use woods and covered approaches, take up defensive positions and generally operate as ordinary infantry in ordinary country. Being very largely countrymen this open-air, open-country work suited them admirably, and in many cases companies and platoons found themselves practising tactical movements on Saturdays and Sundays on the very ground they had been ploughing during the week.

On the alert,
800 years later.

SHROPSHIRE

THE story of Shropshire's section of the western frontier of England is very similar to that of Herefordshire. The borders of both counties ran along the eastern slopes of the Welsh mountains and consequently both had to meet the first shock of retaliatory raids and vengeance-seeking forays by the Welsh – originally the English. These latter had been pushed out of England by early invaders from the Continent in the 500 years before the Romans landed at Deal in AD 55. Invading-occupiers in the succeeding 1,500 years included Romans, Saxons, Danes and Normans. All were brought to a halt by the resisting Welshmen, all had to build hillforts to withstand their counterattacks, all slowly had to form the western frontier of England.

Herefordshire's line of hillforts, described in the chapter on that county, had an advantage not enjoyed by Shropshire; namely, the Malvern Hills. The massive and imposing fortifications there provided an enormous psychological backing to the advanced outpost line thirty-five miles in front.

Iron Age forts

The Welsh foothills come much farther to the east in the southern half of Shropshire than they do in Herefordshire. In the latter county there is a clearly defined low fertile plain between the Welsh mountains and the Malvern Hills, but in Shropshire the whole of its southern half is mountainous. Thus there are no clearly defined areas for defensive works on tactical features, and the lay-out of the defensive Iron Age forts is without pattern. In the southern half of the county they stretch from Clun Forest in the extreme west to Titterstone-Clee and Brown Clee Hills, near Cleobury Mortimer in the east, a distance of twenty-five miles. To the north they reach to Oswestry.

The two counties differ in other respects, although both forming the frontier. Shropshire is more than two-thirds bigger than Herefordshire, indeed it is the largest county in England not bordering on the sea. It has the deep, fast Severn flowing through it, and through its capital of Shrewsbury. Herefordshire has only the mostly sluggish Wye. Shropshire's south-east and eastern sections have become industrialized through the centuries and there is, consequently, a smaller proportion of agricultural land. Very naturally the inhabitants of the far western sections of both counties speak with a pronounced Welsh accent and the names of the villages in these areas often have Celtic names brought over from the Continent by the earliest invaders who settled when it was held up by the Welsh. Villages in the same area often have names beginning with 'Llan . . .', implying that their founders and original inhabitants came down into the Shropshire plain when the peace brought by Edward I in 1282 took effect.

Old Oswestry and the battle of Maserfield

The most spectacular of all the hillforts in Shropshire is Old Oswestry. It covers forty acres and shows, to the skilled eye of the trained archaeologist, that it was built about 250 BC and underwent several alterations. It was first abandoned in AD 45 and is of interest as being reoccupied in the fifth century for use against the Welsh raids after the Romans left England in AD 415. Its tactical position is puzzling in that there is no river, nor even stream, to ford, or to bridge, which might call for protection. Two roads from Wrexham in the north and Whitchurch to the north-east converge close by, but when Old Oswestry was built they were only tracks, if they existed at all. Offa's Dyke runs from north to south just to the west of the town but it was built over a thousand years later than Old Oswestry. Possibly

the fort was brought into active use and refortified by Offa to be a bastion behind his wall. But if this was to be its tactical use, the Dyke should have been farther out to allow its evicted defenders time and space in which to withdraw into the fortress behind them.

The old fort is easily found, its western wall lining the second-class road northward from Oswestry to Weston Rhyn about a mile out of the town. It consists of four ditches with a wall behind each making the outer slope. Rising up from the surrounding meadows it is an imposing sight and the visitor will be struck by the extent of the manual labour that must have been needed to pile up this immense artificial mound. Surprisingly there are no signs of any hollows near by whence the earth could have come, and the inescapable conclusion is that it came from miles away, thereby adding to the already immense labour. The almost flat top is grass-covered and big enough to hold a full-size football pitch.

Hillfort: Old Oswestry covers forty acres. Built c. 250 BC, it was first abandoned in AD 45 and reoccupied in the fifth century for use against Welsh raiders after the Romans had left in AD 415.

In AD 642 the powerful Welsh King, Penda, ravaged the northern part of the county and defeated Oswald, a local chieftain, later a Christian saint, at Old Oswestry at the battle of Maserfield. The site of this battlefield has been identified as a field near the present church of Oswestry, Cae Glas Park today. Oswald was killed in the battle and Penda nailed his body to a cross. The cross was planted in the field, and naturally became known as Oswald's Tree, thus giving Oswestry its present name.

Opposite Offa's Dyke, Llanfair Waterdine.

The Wrekin

Seven miles south-east from Shrewsbury, lying between the roads to Bridgnorth and Wellington, is the last eastward extremity of the Welsh Mountains, the Wrekin. Only sixty feet lower than the Worcestershire Beacon in the Malvern Hills, this isolated little mountain utterly commands the flat country all round it. The basic structure of the fort is a bank just below the summit and encircling it, enclosing seven acres. The protection given by this bank was aided by the artificial scarping of the hill-side below it, the two works together making a very severe obstacle to any troops advancing up the hill. It is possible to drive a car nearly to the top along a narrow road running up the hill from its north-east extremity. The north-west face of the long hill acts as a stop-butt for a modern rifle range near Wrekin Farm. A badly-aimed bullet becoming a ricochet could easily, today, hit one of the lower banks of the prehistoric fort in its upward flight. What a link in military history!

Viroconium (near Wroxeter)

Between the roads A5 and A458, leading south-east from Shrewsbury and half-a-mile north of the village of Wroxeter, lay the Roman town of Viroconium (or Uriconium). There is some evidence, however, that there was a prehistoric settlement on the site. Five second-class roads (tracks, of course, 2,000 years ago) meet there, and the River Severn flows less than half a mile away. The river meanders through flat meadows and it seems likely that a ford existed somewhere near and that the prehistoric site was maintained here to guard such a ford. The Romans certainly established the site very early in their occupation of Shropshire, and used it as a military base prior to their conquest of Wales. They had a river crossing just west of Wroxeter where traces of a wooden bridge were found joining the left bank to the island in the river. This Roman military camp was the headquarters of the Western Command of the invaders until about AD 78 – when it was moved to Chester. Chester is still today the Headquarters of the Western Command of the British Army in England.

There is little to be seen at Viroconium today except one large building, the Roman bath-house and the meeting place of the five roads. A few

The Wrekin, an isolated mountain commanding the surrounding flat country. The fort, consisting of a bank just below the summit enclosing seven acres, is defended by artificial scarping of the hillside below.

Remains of the Roman town of Viroconium near Wroxeter. It was the headquarters of the Roman Western Command until *c.* AD 78 when the command was moved to Chester.

cottages, all surrounded by arable land with its annual ploughing have obliterated the settlement, although the main lines of the streets have been identified by aerial photography. It is of interest that the village church at Wroxeter, though built in Saxon-style architecture has much stone and Roman bricks in its fabric brought from the near-by ruins. (A large proportion of the original building of St Albans Abbey, of the eighth century, was similarly built from the ruins of Verulamium a mile away.)

It is cause for speculation as to why the Roman town had two Latin names, while the village of Wroxeter only half a mile away has a Saxon name including the syllable '. . . xeter', meaning a Roman castle.

Grouped forts

Most of the hilltops in the western part of the county were topped by forts, and there is strong evidence that several groups had their separate tactical unity. Mostly the lesser forts cluster round a bigger one and were linked by still existing footpaths and tracks. One such group is on and around Pontesbury – between Shrewsbury and Bishop's Castle on the A488. Here there are four hillforts in the immediate vicinity, all excepting Callow Hill, just east of Minsterley, being very difficult of access, through woods and up very steep escarpments. But Callow Hill is close to a by-road running east from Minsterley, and demands a fair walk with little climbing. Regrettably there is not much to see. There was a trackway running from Pontesford north-west to the Breidden Hill group, and the second-class road running through Westbury is almost certainly that track in use today. The word Pontesbury is curious. There is no bridge or ford over or through any river or stream within one mile.

The hillfort on Titterstone Clee Hill had the outer ditch excavated from solid rock, the spoil being used as an inner rampart above the ditch. Brown Clee Hill has several summits. The most northerly, Abdon Burf, is 1,700 feet high, and has a massive fort but has been largely destroyed by quarrying. In this group and a mile and a half to the south-west is Nordybank Hill (overlooking the village of Clee St Margaret) also crowned by a fort. The saddle between these two large hills bears the engaging name of Abdon Liberty. Norton Camp, almost 1,000 feet high, lies on the most southerly tip of Wenlock Edge. It encloses about ten acres, is completely circular, is now almost surrounded by trees and is the most difficult of access in the whole county. Immediately to the west of Church Stretton lies a long broad feature, the Long Mynd. Its highest point, Pole Bank, is 1,700 feet high, and along it there are five hillforts or at least earthworks, suggesting military defences. All are difficult of access, but that on Bodbury Hill overshadowing the golf course on its northern slopes makes a reasonable to walk from the 'fifteenth' fairway.

There are many other hillforts in Shropshire not mentioned here, but all are similar to those described and are mostly difficult to reach. All are rewarding to the active young hill-climbing historian.

Apart from Viroconium and Wroxeter, the Romans left little evidence of any military works in Shropshire. There was Mediolanium, now identified as Whitchurch in the north of the county, which had a military fort, built probably only as a staging post on the road from Viroconium to Chester, today the A5113. All traces of this fort have disappeared, but the modern High Street follows the line of the original Roman road, while the basic street-plan today reflects the Roman town-plan of the first century AD.

An unidentified fortified settlement

Two miles south of Cleobury North – on the Bridgnorth-Ludlow road – lies a very small isolated hamlet, Aston Botterell. A quarter of a mile to its south there stood until 1844 an even smaller hamlet, Bold. Here there was a very old chapel dating from about 1150 (the subject of a charming watercolour painted by the Rev. Mr Williams in 1790 and now hanging in the Shrewsbury Public Library). The chapel was the centre of the hamlet which has now disappeared. Around it are the extensive remains of earthworks, particularly to the south of the site of the chapel. Primarily they are the remains of a pre-Norman Conquest settlement, but on further examination there seems to be a military atmosphere. The shape and layout of the surrounding wall suggest fortifications.

The siting of a little isolated church is often of significance. Occupying an eminence, no matter how minor, it can usually be presumed to have been the centre of a community that has shifted elsewhere, been dispossessed, or failed economically. At Bold it clearly was the centre of a community, and in the Dark Ages and early Norman era, churches were not only the place of Christian worship but also of sanctuary in cases of attack. Bold shows the site of the church, the village centre, the site of the village all round it, and outside that the defensive walls. All are or were quite evident. It is surprising however that there is little local knowledge of the walls or their defensive nature, the ex-village is not marked on the 1-inch Ordnance Survey map – and on the $2\frac{1}{2}$-inch map there is only one large building shewn, with 'chapel, (site of)' alongside the building. Bold seems to have just collapsed, died and disintegrated.

The Dark Ages are nowhere darker than in Shropshire. Very little is known of what occurred between the collapse of the Roman administration in AD 415 and about AD 640. This obscurity may contain the secret of Bold.

For the less active touring historian a visit to the fort on the south-west corner of Wart Hill is quite easy. From Craven Arms northward along the road to Church Stretton – the A49 – turn left half a mile out of the little town along an easily negotiated road signposted to Lydbury North or Edgton. Two miles along this road Wart Hill will be seen on the right. At its far end the car is but 200 yards from the fort and the walking, although uphill, is by no means steep or strenuous.

Offa's Dyke in Shropshire

The prehistoric and Roman settlements to be found in Shropshire should not be left without making a visit to Offa's Dyke. Starting from near Prestatyn on the estuary of the Dee in Flintshire it runs more or less due south to the mouth of the river Wye opposite Chepstow, a distance of nearly 120 miles, and is the most tangible legacy from the Dark Ages to be seen today. On its journey southward it runs in and out of England, although it would be more correct to say that the western boundaries of Shropshire, Herefordshire and Gloucestershire, the western frontier of England, frequently cross and recross it in their convolutions. The longest continuous section of the whole Dyke is in the south-west corner of Shropshire, where it can easily be seen and walked along. Here it is generally about eighteen feet from the bottom of the ditch to the summit of the great bank. The ditch is usually on the outer, western, side although farther to the south this ditch sometimes appears on the inner side. Generally it follows contour lines rather than hill-tops or ridges, and is easily walked.

As was seen in the chapter on Herefordshire, the Dyke was built for two purposes. Firstly, King Offa of Mercia intended it as a landmark to show the Welsh exactly where his territory ended and theirs began. He wanted no misunderstanding on the matter and so designed a landmark that could not be moved. In addition, if the Welsh were foolish enough to descend on his kingdom he would have this ready-made defensive ditch available for his troops to occupy.

William I's defence system

After the Conquest of 1066 and the publication, if such a word may be used, of the Domesday Book in 1085, the policy of William the Conqueror regarding the Western Frontier of England (described in the chapter on Herefordshire), applied equally to Shropshire. In short, he saw from the Domesday Book that there was a large number of English great houses along the English side of the frontier. None of them could be reasonably expected to be more friendly to him and his invading army than anywhere else in England. Out in the far west country they might well combine against him and – an additional danger – might also collectively join the Welsh across the border only a few miles away. Together they could threaten his occupation, his army, even his throne. Consequently he dispossessed many of them, replacing them with Norman knights of whose integrity he was sure, and, to whom he wished to show gratitude. These were the Marcher Lords. He encouraged them to extend, and then fortify, their new homes and so had them develop along his dangerous frontier a chain of strong points at the expense of the new owners.

William's method of distribution of these manors differed in Shropshire from the method he had used in Herefordshire. In Herefordshire there were the two distinct and quite separate tactical areas, the last most easterly foothills of the Welsh mountains, and thirty-five miles behind them the Malvern Hills. On the former the forward outpost line had been built and held for centuries, while the main stopline had been along the latter.

In Shropshire there were no two distinct tactical defence areas, the last of the Welsh foothills reaching right across the county. In Herefordshire he had the insight to see that the foothills and their forts could be combined tactically with the newly fortified manors, creating some local military entity and thus perhaps a local *esprit de corps.* In their mutual interest the groups would stick together, far out near the frontier as they were.

Three great Marcher Lords

In Shropshire William found the hills and their hillforts spread right across the county, from the Welsh border eastward back to the present Staffordshire border, a distance of nearly forty miles, and he could not trust this great mass of fortifications and potential areas of intrigue and resistance to remain continuously facing west against the ever-present Welsh aggression, and not to face east and the centre of his kingdom. Accordingly he placed in possession only three great Norman knights. Roger de Montgomery was in Shrewsbury, Roger de Lacy in Ludlow, and Robert de Say in Clun. These three great Marcher Lords forced all Welsh raids back firmly into the mountains and ruled their considerable territories like petty princes; they were almost deputy-kings. Soon a string of lesser castles sprang up along the border, none so powerful as their counterparts in Herefordshire. All were held firmly in the grip of the three commanders on the spot, the great Marcher Lords.

These lesser castles, of which over 150 have been identified in Shropshire, are or were not very imposing. They were usually of the motte-and-baily type. The motte was a mound, usually circular, whose sides were faced with timber or stone. It lay in the bailey, an open flat space with no cover for any advance across it against the motte. The outer perimeter of the bailey was walled and with the ditch outside it intended to be the first line of defence. Nearly all have been eroded by the winter weather of 900 years, some are tree-covered, the outer ditches have silted up and in some cases the mottes have been deliberately levelled to allow uninterrupted ploughing.

The castles of the Marches

The bigger castles are of great interest. Stokesay Castle, one mile south of Craven Arms, must have first mention, being the best specimen of a fortified manor in England. Parts of it date from the early twelfth century. It cannot or should not be called a castle. It was not intended for aggressive military defence, an item in a broad pattern of similar buildings, but rather as a fine family manor house. Its walls and moat were solely for self-defence.

Stokesay Castle, the best specimen of a fortified manor in England. Parts of the building date from the twelfth century. Given to the Marcher Lord, Picôt de Say, Stokesay was held for Charles I in the Civil War but capitulated when threatened by the Parliamentarians and so escaped damage.

One of the three great Marcher Lords, Picot de Say, was given this manor of Stoke by William I. Picot was one of those encouraged to develop their manor houses and in addition he built a church close by. Parts of this church survive in the existing building, and the doorway is clearly Norman. Another Stoke existed in Shropshire in the twelfth century near Market Drayton and to distinguish it from this one with its castle the latter had its owner's name – Say – added, hence Stokesay.

The original gate house, crenellated by royal authority in 1291, is a magnificent edifice but for four centuries, the main entrance has been a beautiful Elizabethan half-timbered building of two storeys. Its great oak door is loopholed for musketry. Despite the castle's professed negative defensive intention, it is nevertheless strongly fortified and the moat, with its inner wall of eight or nine feet, is a formidable obstacle on the north side.

Overlooking Stokesay Castle from the east, and only half a mile away is Norton Camp, at the extreme south-west tip of Wenlock Edge. It is admittedly the most difficult of access of all prehistoric hillforts in Shropshire – even by the most active historian.

Stokesay was held for King Charles in the Civil War but capitulated to the Parliamentarians when threatened and suffered no damage from artillery fire.

Shrewsbury Castle was built in 1068 by Roger de Montgomery, as a private residence for himself and then extended and fortified as his part in the defence of the frontier of England. There is evidence however that an older defensive building had stood on the site before the Conquest.

When Roger first built his castle one hundred and one small peasants' cottages were demolished to make room for the great building. Its main entrance today, a Norman gateway, is the oldest part and what remains is largely thirteenth century, erected by Edward I. In 1790 the famous engineer, Thomas Telford, who built the Clifton and Menai Straits suspension bridges, converted the castle into a dwelling-house, and consequently it lost much of its character. Perhaps the most striking fact about it is its position. At Shrewsbury the Severn makes a great loop around the town and the land enclosed is, at its widest, nearly three quarters of a mile across, and over half a mile from north to south. However the two arms of the river nearly meet to the north of the town and the neck of land separating them is only 300 yards wide. In this neck Montgomery built the castle, showing his tactical eye for country. Both flanks of the castle and its rear are guarded, indeed blocked, by the Severn, never less than fifty yards wide and frequently eighty, while a mile to the north is a low eminence. Of no tactical value to an attacker against the castle, it provided the defenders with an excellent observation post to the north.

Clun Castle is a magnificent spectacle. It stands on a considerable hill within a crook of the river Clun, the little town of today being just to its east. Walking westward along Newport Street a superb view is obtained. It was built by Robert de Say, one of the three great Marcher Lords, soon after the Conquest and largely extended and more heavily fortified as a result of William's policy towards his great nobles and their homes along the western frontier. There is evidence that long before Say built it there had been a moated stronghold of Saxon times on this site. Today there remains an impressive Norman keep, whose sides seem to spring into the sky when viewed from Newport Street. The keep is on the top of a great mound eighty feet high, with walls eleven feet thick. The main door was to the south with a staircase built within the wall. Two great round bastions, with a wall between them containing a fireplace and two fourteenth-century windows, are, with the great tower, practically the only masonry surviving above ground today. Around two thirds of the eminence on which it stands flows the river Clun, twenty yards wide, guarding the castle from the west and south. Fast flowing, between banks usually three feet high, the river made a serious obstacle to an attacker. With its size, tactical position guarded by the river, and its own eminence it was one of the most formidable defensive castles in the west of England. The visitor should not leave Clun until he has inspected the bridge over the river Clun on its way to join the river Teme. This ancient saddle-backed bridge has five low arches separated by projecting angle piers, built to allow pedestrians to stand aside when meeting a vehicle on the bridge. Also before leaving Clun the historian should drive three miles west along the B4868 road to the little village of Newcastle. Just short of the village Offa's Dyke crosses the road and it can be followed with great ease on foot in either direction. The area is known as Clun Forest but it is, in reality, open moorland and the great Dyke can be seen stretching away for some miles. Here it is the longest unbroken section throughout its entire length.

Lydbury North is a hamlet two and a half miles south-east of Bishop's Castle (five miles north of Clun). Another two miles to the east is Plowden Hall. Today it is a half-timbered Elizabethan mansion, owned by the Plowden family who have been in possession since the Conquest. It was in its time a fortified Norman manor, and there are still traces of the original fortifications. The first Plowden to be known by name as an individual was alive in 1180. One mile south of Lydbury North is Walcot, an imposing red brick mansion. Although of no military importance or connection, it is of interest in that it contains a large number of Indian curiosities of the first Lord Clive, the great soldier-civilian who did so much to consolidate the British power in India.

Ludlow Castle is a magnificent sight from any angle. It is a perfect specimen of a ruin that requires no imagination to visualize its lay-out, its former beauty, its imposing majesty.

It was one of the great manors given by William the Conqueror to his favourites, to hold and to fortify. Roger de Lacy received Ludlow and his castle, lying on one of the most eastern foothills of the Welsh mountains saw much service in repelling the Welsh invasions.

Henry I checks the barons

Henry I, the Conqueror's fourth and ablest, son succeeded his brother, William Rufus in AD 1100. He at once set about curbing the growing power of the great nobles, and in particular gained control of several of the Shropshire castles. But after a strong

Opposite Clun Castle, built by the Marcher Lord, Robert de Say, on the site of a moated Saxon stronghold. The keep has walls eleven feet thick and stands on a mound eighty feet high. Guarded on west and south by the fast flowing river Clun, twenty yards wide beneath deep banks, this was one of the most formidable defensive castles in the west of England.

and fair reign of thirty-five years, he was succeeded by Stephen. The direct descent of the crown was to Henry's daughter, Matilda, but the majority of the Great Council of Nobles would not accept that a woman could be a monarch, and offered the crown to Stephen, grandson of the Conqueror.

Plowden Hall, a much restored Elizabethan mansion on the site of a fortified Norman manor – of which traces of the original fortifications can still be seen.

Opposite Ludlow Castle and the Old Bridge. The great manor of Ludlow was given by William the Conqueror to Roger de Lacy and the castle on the most eastern foothills of the Welsh mountains saw much service in repelling Welsh invasions.

Matilda: Ludlow Castle

The country was split into factions supporting either Stephen the monarch, or Matilda, the rightful claimant, and the 'nineteen long winters' ensued, when 'Christ and his saints slept'. Generally the Shropshire barons supported Matilda and her undoubted claim to the throne of England. Many of them, also, welcomed a chance to engage some of their fellow nobles and wipe off old scores. Ludlow was held for Matilda, its defences were strengthened and in 1138 Stephen himself led an army into Shropshire and besieged the castle. He failed to capture it, several attempts to breach the defences being repelled, understandably when its position is observed.

It occupies a magnificent tactical position on high ground overlooking a distinct curve in the River Teme. The cliffs fall steeply to the river on the west and north sides and the castle is virtually impregnable in this direction. The cliff continues eastward, beyond the end of the castle wall, before sinking to the level of the surrounding fields after it has provided a discouraging obstacle to any attack from the north-east.

As usual a town grew up outside the castle walls and at its main gate. Eventually walls were built round the town in about 1230, a hundred years after the siege, and thus the castle was further defended by the very existence of the town. No attacking general likes to fight in streets or to advance through them.

The castle is roughly circular, with its main gate in the eastern segment facing directly down Castle Square, the High Street, and King Street, a splendid vista of nearly a quarter of a mile. The outer bailey within the main castle walls is very large, almost 200 yards long and big enough for a moderate-sized football pitch. Overlooking it from the west is the inner bailey behind which the cliffs fall steeply away. Within the inner bailey are the remains of an unusual circular Norman chapel, and a well eighty-five feet deep.

Ludlow Castle has seen much history. Edward IV used it as a residence for his two young sons when he came to the throne, and it was here that the elder prince was proclaimed King Edward V on his father's death in 1483. But he was never to reign,

Ludlow Castle: the Postern tower from the keep. The background shows the height of the castle above its surrounding country. The octagonal grating covers the ancient well of unknown depth. The water-level never varies.

Ludlow Castle; the inner bailey. The circular building is a Norman chapel. Here worshipped Arthur, elder son of Henry VII, when he spent his honeymoon here with Catherine of Aragon. After Arthur's death Catherine married his brother who became Henry VIII.

being hurried with his young brother, Richard, to the Tower by their uncle Richard of Gloucester who was soon to proclaim himself Richard III. In the Tower both young princes disappeared.

Henry VII, who was to defeat Richard III at Bosworth in 1485, had two sons. Arthur the elder married Catherine of Aragon and the young couple spent their honeymoon in Ludlow Castle. On Arthur's death Catherine was married to his brother, Henry, later to be the notorious Henry VIII. He sent their daughter, Mary, to live in Ludlow Castle for some years, perhaps the happiest period of her tragic life. All these young 'royals' must have worshipped in the circular Norman chapel in the inner bailey. Ludlow next appears in history in the Civil War, when it was the last stronghold in England to submit to Cromwell. It surrendered only because some of its garrison had been bribed to sow disaffection among their fellows.

The main approach to Ludlow from the south crosses Ludlow Bridge, which is nearly 700 years old. It replaced an older bridge dating from Norman times.

Of all castles or fortified Norman manors in Shropshire, Ludlow is pre-eminent in interest and should at all costs be visited. Cars can be parked very near the main gate, in Castle Square.

In 1158 King Stephen, having failed to capture Ludlow Castle, moved on to Shrewsbury where he succeeded in capturing the castle there (and hanged 100 men of the garrison on the spot).

Acton Burnell is another ruined castle. It lies four miles south-west of Cressage (eight miles south-east of Shrewsbury), and is picturesque but little more. It was a tall rectangular building, with towers still standing at the four corners. The main outer walls enclosed a great room eighty feet by sixty, now open to the sky, and turfed. Local legend claims that it was in this great hall that the first Parliament met, consisting of the monarch, Edward I, great nobles,

and elected burgesses from each county and town. But this attractive legend cannot be true. The election by the people of their own representatives to govern them was the direct result of Simon de Montfort's great victory at Lewes in 1264, eighteen years before. Edward I did not make his state visit to Shropshire until 1283. It is not impossible that he did in fact hold a parliament at Acton Burnell. But it could not have been the first.

For the next two hundred years the history of Shropshire consists of raids from the Welsh mountains across the frontier of England in the county. Oswestry, Ellesmere, Shrewsbury, Bridgnorth and several of the lesser castles and settlements all suffered attacks, sieges, and sackings. Reliefs followed and the raiders were driven back but the west and south parts of Shropshire were ablaze, or likely to be, at any moment. The broad result of these terrible 200 years in Shropshire, and to a lesser extent in Herefordshire, was the crystallization of a county spirit to the east of the frontier, and a psychological and material withdrawal of the Welsh into their own mountains.

Acton Burnell Castle. Edward I is said to have held an early parliament here.

THE BATTLE OF SHREWSBURY

In 1399 occurred the event that led to the Wars of the Roses which lasted from 1455 to 1485, and produced Shropshire's greatest and best known military engagement, the Battle of Shrewsbury, 1403.

Richard II, son of the Black Prince and grandson of Edward III, who died before his father, was one of England's really bad kings. He was weak, far from intelligent, violent-tempered, and in his later years, tyrannical. His cousin, Henry Bolingbroke, son of John of Gaunt, Duke of Lancaster, fourth son of Edward III, raised a rebellion against him, and he was deposed, being placed for safety in Pontefract Castle, where he disappeared, presumed murdered. Bolingbroke seized the throne and was crowned, King Henry IV, the first of the Lancastrian monarchs. This brutal and unconstitutional event is considered to be a turning point in the history of English monarchy, showing that the throne is not entirely hereditary but partly selective. Six monarchs, found wanting in capacity or unwilling in spirit, have vacated the throne. Richard II, Edward II, Henry VI and Charles I were found either wanting or unco-operative with their people and were either murdered or executed. James II ran away, while in this century the abdication of Edward VIII remains in the memory of many.

This usurpation of the throne by Henry IV caused great unrest in the country. The king's supporters, the Lancastrians, had serious rivals in the descendants of the Duke of York, third son of Edward III, and the plots and counterplots to safeguard the position of the king or to place his rivals, the Yorks, on the throne bedevilled English politics for many years.

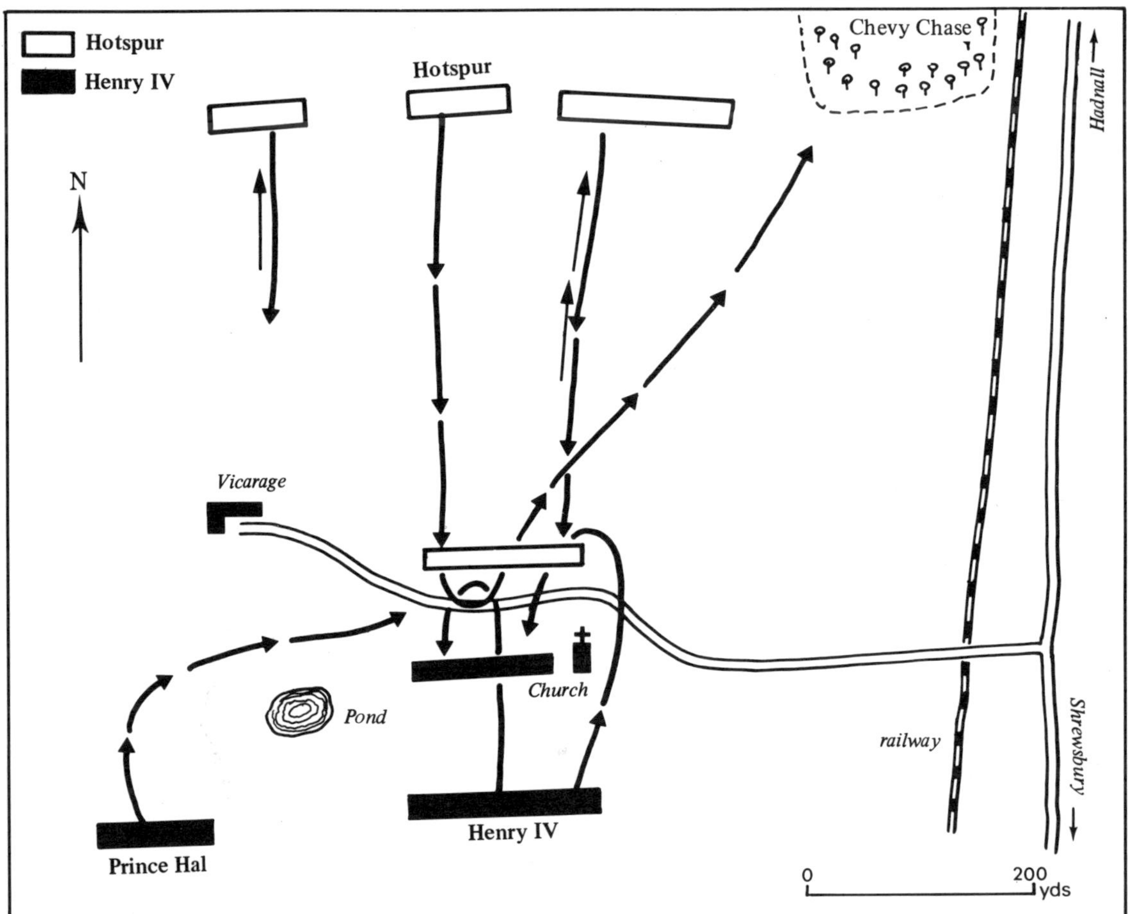

The Battle of Shrewsbury.

Three families unite against Henry IV

The great family of Percy of Northumberland, perhaps the most powerful non-royal family in England, together with their tenants had been the chief supporters of Henry's action against Richard II. But in the unrest of Henry's accession they quarrelled with him on a trivial matter concerning the exchange of some prisoners-of-war after a minor battle on the Scottish Border. At once they formed a conspiracy with the equally powerful families of Glendower of Wales, and the Mortimers of Shropshire, and marched south to join forces against the king.

Henry marched up to Shrewsbury where his young son, Shakespeare's famous Prince Hal, later the romantic Henry V of Agincourt, had a small army. Hearing that 'Hotspur', Percy's son, with an army of 10,000 had left Chester moving southward, Henry and young Hal took up a position facing north along some high ground now known as Battlefield, three miles north of Shrewsbury, to bar Hotspur's road. Their line ran from the present A49, Shrewsbury-Hadnall road, near the junction with the third-class road running due west to where the church now stands, and passed one hundred yards south.

As Henry's men were taking up their positions Hotspur's army was occupying considerably higher ground opposite, about 500 yards away along the southern edge of Ash Walk Coppice. It covered a frontage of 800 yards and lay along the ridge 400 yards north of the present church. When all was ready the Abbot of Shrewsbury passed from one army to the other hoping to arrange some settlement of the argument, but to no avail.

The Royal army advanced, and a heavy exchange of fire took place. The king's long-bowmen halted

Shrewsbury Castle, built by Roger de Montgomery *c.* 1068, stands in a commanding position in the loop of the Severn. In 1790 it was renovated by the engineer Telford as his private residence.

and opened fire when they reached a line just to the north of the present church. Hotspur's men returned the fire skilfully and effectively and greatly dismayed the Royal regulars. They had expected a walk-over against an army which, only recently recruited, had little training and was merely composed of family retainers from the three great families, Percies, Mortimers and Glendowers.

Hotspur's counter-attack routed

The aim of Henry's men became ragged and their rate of fire slowed. After a heavy exchange of arrows the Royal army withdrew in some disorder. Hotspur seized his advantage and advanced down the slope, his men-at-arms catching many of the archers. At the bottom of the rise Henry's men stopped and faced about, when a general mêlée ensued around the ponds in front of and on either side of the present church and the house shewn on the modern map as 'vicarage'. Hotspur, with thirty knights, tried to hack his way through the fight to reach and dispatch the king, as had happened at Hastings, but Henry's chief-of-staff saw the possibility and persuaded the king to leave the danger zone. Meanwhile, Prince Hal's division out on the left had suffered little from arrow fight and now saw a chance to play some part. They advanced and attacked Hotspur's right flank between the westernmost pond and the vicarage. Pushing on, they got behind the enemy who were thus threatened from the rear, their right, and from the undefeated king's army, with which they were closely embroiled to their front. In the course of this now indescribable chaos Hotspur was felled by an arrow and as usual in medieval battles, the elimination of a leader resulted in wholesale collapse and retreat. Henry advanced again and sending his cavalry in, pursued Hotspur's men for three miles, to total victory.

The battlefield

Today the site of the battle is easy to find, visit and see, the best viewpoint being the lane from the church to the vicarage. The pond is still there, about thirty yards by twenty, and is never dry even after the longest drought. On its bank are two hoary gnarled oaks, possibly young trees in 1403.

The church was built by Henry IV in 1408 in memory of the fallen of both sides. Much of the original stained glass remains, and high up in the clerestory are very old replicas of the shields of Henry, his son young Hal, and about twenty of his knights. Outside, high up on the eastern gable, is a carved stone statue of Henry. It has never been removed and is much weather-beaten.

Apart from the church, the vicarage, and the next farm higher up the ridge, all is as it was in 1403. Hedges have appeared, of course. (Hedges are quite a modern invention, not having been used or planted until the eighteenth century.) There is no need to speculate at the battlefield of Shrewsbury, all the features are there to see.

Three quarters of a mile to the north of the church is a large wood called Chevy Chase but there seems to be no connection between this unusual name and the battle fought 170 miles away in Northumberland fifteen years previously. Equally curious is the fact that at the Northumberland battlefield there is no wood, moor, hill or stream of that name in the district and up there the local people do not know why the battle was so called. At the battle of Shrewsbury the defeated Scots were in fact 'chased' through this wood by Henry IV's cavalry and the suspicion is inescapable that the author of 'The Ballad of Chevy Chase' confused the two battles. Perhaps Otterburn has been living in a false notoriety for six hundred years, while Shrewsbury has modestly accepted the lesser limelight.

Ludlow

Shropshire appeared only briefly in the Wars of the Roses. After the defeat of the Lancastrians at Blore Heath in 1459, the Yorkist army marched on Ludlow, where it encamped in the meadows at Ludford, a suburb to the south of Ludlow. Here their entrenched position enabled them to repel the Lancastrians again. But treachery in the Yorkist ranks caused them to waver and during the night they disintegrated and escaped in the darkness. The Lancastrians crossed the river and entered the town plundering it and the great castle. They then marched on and out of the county into Herefordshire to their defeat at Mortimer's Cross. For the next 180 years Shropshire saw no military events of any kind.

In 1642, however, Shropshire again saw soldiers. King Charles I, having declared war on his parliament at Nottingham, marched to Shrewsbury where he held a grand review. He then turned for London marching through Bridgnorth and Kidderminster. On his way he won the battle of Edgehill in Warwickshire. No great battles in the Civil War were fought in the county but there were plenty of cavalry skirmishes. Market Drayton, Lilleshall, Whittington, Stokesay, Knockin Heath, and High Ercall all saw these quite unimportant little affairs. The site of each fracas is unknown.

The Old Lion, Shrewsbury, where Henry VII slept before going on to the Battle of Bosworth, 1485.

Above right The Boscobel Oak which can be seen today is a descendant of the Royal Oak in which King Charles hid. By 1661 the original tree had been rifled of its boughs by souvenir hunters. Boscobel House is among the trees to the right.

Right Room in Boscobel House showing the trap door.

Below 'Boscobel House with White Ladies and the Boscobel Oak.' Painted for James II after the Restoration, by Robert Streater. The painting is now in Hampton Court Palace.

Generally Shropshire was Royalist, and the vast majority of the great houses were strongholds for the king. But the Parliamentary forces gradually occupied the whole county, and every great house eventually succumbed, Ludlow Castle being the last to give in.

The only remaining military event to occur in the county in the Civil War was to be the march of King Charles II on his way to the battle of Worcester in 1651. Charles had just lost the battle of Dunbar but was determined to be crowned king of England on English soil having landed in Scotland. He led a Scottish army southward to Carlisle where he was proclaimed king. He marched on through Lancaster and Preston to Chester, and entered Shropshire at Whitchurch, passing through Newport and Tong on the way to his defeat at Worcester and escape to Boscobel four miles to the east of Tong. Boscobel House, where he hid is open to the public in the summer and is of great interest on account of the hiding-places in the walls which can still be seen. In the field near by stands the famed Royal Oak, a descendant of the original tree in which the king took refuge.

Beginnings of a local force

After the Civil War little of military importance occurred in Shropshire until the two attempts of the old Pretender in 1715 and the young Pretender in 1745, to recapture the throne of England. In 1715 there was much fear in the county that the attempt might succeed, and consequently 'a regiment of foot, and horse, were raised to guard Shrewsbury, while several passages through the walls were stopped up, and existing gates fortified'. But nothing happened, the rebels from Scotland only reaching Preston in Lancashire where they were defeated and captured.

The other invasion by Scottish rebels under Bonny Prince Charlie, the Young Pretender, in 1745, was more serious. After his victory over English Regular regiments at Prestonpans, Prince Charles marched southward, making for London, and in fact penetrated the Midlands as far as Derby, only fifty-five miles from Shrewsbury. There was much greater consternation than in 1715, and as a result there was wild confusion in the town when rumours spread of the Scots being much nearer than they were in fact. Many of the inhabitants left hurriedly, camping out in villages to the west, and the local volunteer regiment of foot was mobilized. However, this unit, being very ill-disciplined and hearing the rumours of the approach of the rebels, also left the town with all their baggage. On hearing that the rebels had turned back at Derby, and were no longer a menace, the local unit returned to its post of duty.

SHROPSHIRE'S OWN REGIMENTS

Ten years after Shrewsbury's alarm over the '45, a very different state of affairs arose in the county. A new Regular regiment was born in 1755.

Following the disbandment of Cromwell's New Model Army in 1661 the formation of new Regular regiments began and by 1754 fifty-two regiments had been raised, still existing today, although many are amalgamated. But there were not enough. The struggles with France on the Continent, and in India called for ever more regiments and in 1755 authority was given to raise the 53rd Regiment of Foot in Shropshire. The officer appointed for this task was a Colonel Whitmore, of Apley near Bridgnorth. Two hundred years later, to celebrate the Regiment's bi-centenary a ceremonial parade was held at Bridgnorth when the Mayor bestowed the Freedom of the Borough on the Regiment. Three of Colonel Whitmore's descendants were on the platform at the parade. In 1785 the name of the county was included in the Regiment's official title.

Four years after the birth of the 53rd in Shropshire, a regiment was born in Buckinghamshire, the 85th King's Light Infantry, the first regiment in the British Army to be called, and drilled as, Light Infantry. In the Cardwell reforms of the British Infantry in 1881 these two units were linked into a two-battalions regiment, to become The King's Shropshire Light Infantry.

The 53rd at Salamanca

In its earlier days the greatest achievement of the 53rd was at the battle of Salamanca in the Peninsular War in 1812. After the retreat to Corunna and embarkation there, Wellington had been sent out to Portugal as commander-in-chief with massive reinforcements. Advancing north-east from Lisbon for

Band of the King's Shropshire Light Infantry, *c.* 1880.

nearly three years he gradually pushed the French armies back into Spain, where, north-west of Madrid, he came up with Marmont, Napoleon's youngest marshal – his personal friend since their cadetship days at Brienne, and undoubtedly a most able general. Wellington had seven divisions, the 53rd being in the 6th Division.

The British army's objective was twofold, to make for and secure the exit from Spain into France through the narrow gap between the Mediterranean and the western end of the Pyrenees, and thus prevent reinforcements coming down to Marmont and secondly to meet and defeat the French when and wherever they were found.

By mid-July in scorching weather Marmont held the town of Salamanca with Wellington threatening him from the west. Almost surrounded, Marmont evacuated the town, and gathered his force together in the hills to the south-east. Wellington occupied the town and moved out to occupy the nearer group of hills. His left rested on a low ridge, ending on the considerable hill, the Lesser Arapile. The 53rd were holding the northern face of this hill, while opposite it across the valley on the Greater Arapile stood Marmont's strong right wing. To the right of the 6th Division the remainder of Wellington's army was deployed on low hills for almost two miles.

Marmont started the attack by a feint on his right against the 6th Division while moving his mass to his left, to outflank the British right. The feint attack was held by the 6th Division but the 53rd suffered considerably by long-range artillery fire, and was forced to evacuate its exposed position. It then reformed square on its fresh ground, and met and repulsed a strong enemy cavalry attack. It advanced again and reoccupied its original position, restoring the left flank. The French withdrew, devoting all the attention to their grandiose left flank move to encircle the British right. After the crisis of the cavalry attack, Colonel Bingham, who commanded the 53rd for twelve years from 1805 to

1817, led the Battalion back to its original position personally carrying the King's Colour. There is little doubt that had the 53rd broken or even retreated farther the enemy would have turned his feint attack into a real one, and thereby with his now developing left flank attack threatened the British army with encirclement. Marmont's main attack round the British right flank now looked like being successful. But he overstretched his army, making too big a wheel and leaving gaps in his centre. Wellington saw his chance, and ordered his 5th Division in the centre to advance down the hill and into the enemy. The French paused, badly shaken, and Wellington sent forward his 3rd Division on to the enemy's very exposed left flank. It crumpled, and two and a half French divisions left the field. Marmont was badly wounded by a long-range stray cannon ball, losing an arm and having two ribs broken.

The KSLI returned to England at the end of the Peninsular War, and was not present at Waterloo nor part of the army of occupation in Paris.

Links with Napoleon

On the abdication of Napoleon and his capture by the British after Waterloo, he was sent to St Helena for permanent incarceration, and the KSLI was detailed to accompany him as Guard Regiment.

Colonel Bingham was still in command of the KSLI and became acquainted with the Emperor. They dined with each other privately and Napoleon was Regimental Guest at a guest-night.

In 1816 Sir Hudson Lowe came out as Governor and made himself extremely unpopular with the civilians of the island, with the soldiers and with Napoleon, whom he treated with quite unnecessary strictness, and with poor manners. The Emperor refused to receive him, declined an invitation to dinner at Plantation House, and said, publicly, 'I'll dine only with the red-coats.'

Captain Poppleton of the KSLI acted as ADC for some time to Napoleon who gave him a gold snuff-box to show his appreciation not only of the young officer but of the Regiment. Most regrettably this little snuff-box, left in his will to the KSLI by Captain Poppleton, was lost in a fire in Hong Kong in 1892. Poppleton managed to secure a lock of Napoleon's hair, presumably by entering his bedroom immediately after the barber had left. This, too, Poppleton left to the Regiment and is today in the Regimental Museum.

This was not the only link between Shropshire and the great military leader. A less important connection and of no military consequence occurred in 1810, in the heyday of Napoleon's reign as Emperor. Lucien Bonaparte, by far the ablest of Napoleon's brothers, had a violent disagreement with the Emperor. Despite many pleas from his mother and his sisters, Lucien refused to be reconciled, and realizing that he had no political future in France he sailed with his wife for America. Passing through the Mediterranean their ship was captured by a British warship and they were taken into Plymouth. From here they were moved to Shropshire where for a few weeks the Earl of Powis entertained them in great luxury at his country seat near Ludlow. Lucien then bought an estate at Thorngrove in Worcestershire where he and his family lived for nearly five years, enjoying country pursuits and hospitality, and taking some part in local affairs. After the collapse of France following her defeat at Waterloo, and eventually the death of Napoleon at St Helena, the Bonaparte family was allowed to leave England. They settled in Italy where Lucien died in 1840.

World War 1

In August 1914 the 1st Battalion of the KSLI was stationed, again with the 6th Division, in Ireland at Tipperary. As it eventually marched along the straight, apparently interminable French roads, it must have sung with much feeling the most popular marching song the British infantry ever had.

The 6th Division was not ordered to France until late August and so missed Mons, Le Cateau, the Great Retreat and the Marne, going into action for the first time at the Aisne and the beginning of trench warfare. The 1st KSLI remained with the 6th Division in France throughout the war.

The 2nd Battalion – the old 85th – came home from India in August 1914, and after serving in France until November 1915 went with the 27th Division to hold Salonika, where it remained until the Armistice. The mosquito caused far more casualties than the Bulgars.

The 4th Territorial battalion, from Shrewsbury, received a unique distinction in June 1918. Only 300 strong it had been ordered to counter-attack the Germans on a recently captured hill. Brilliantly successful they checked the main enemy advance and thereby saved the left flank of the 5th French Army. For this the battalion as a unit was awarded the Croix de Guerre Avec Palme, the medal being pinned on the Regimental Colours on ceremonial parades. It is the only unit in the British Army to be decorated as a unit.

Men of the 7th Shropshire Light Infantry returning from the trenches, near Toutencourt, 18 May 1917.

The 6th Battalion, raised entirely in the town of Shrewsbury, aptly and accurately calling itself the Shrewsbury Pals, had an extraordinary officer as CO who took over command immediately after the battle of Loos in September 1915. By the end of the war in 1918 he had won the DSO and three bars, sharing this distinction with only four other officers in the army. He became Brigade Commander in 1918 being recommended for the VC. This final honour was, however, withheld on the grounds that he had gone too far forward in leading his men, unnecessarily endangering his valuable life. After the war he lived to reach the age of 100, dying in 1967.

Another interesting commanding officer was Colonel Denys Reitz, who commanded the 7th Battalion. He was the author of *Commando* and *Trekking On*. A Boer, he had fought against the British at the age of seventeen under General Smuts in the Anglo–Boer war. He never visited Shropshire.

World War II and the Home Guard

In World War II the KSLI had a curious distinction. The 1st Battalion, in the 1st Division in France from September 1939 to the evacuation at Dunkirk, was the last battalion to embark, its last platoon firing at the German advanced troops while running down the five-foot jetty to the boats. Almost four years later, the 2nd Battalion in the 3rd Division was the first battalion to land on D-Day in Normandy on 6 June 1944.

Shropshire, the biggest county in England having no border on the sea, has its large population of 900,000 in two differing conditions. The four big towns of Shrewsbury, Oswestry, Bridgnorth and Ludlow, and five lesser ones, accommodate less than one seventh of the population. The remainder live in villages, hamlets, and often widely separated estates, small houses, or cottages. There is, consequently, a considerable feudal atmosphere in the country districts. This has bred an intense local and county spirit often springing from a respect (or perhaps a vague obedience) to the 'big house' and the gentry. It was indeed fertile ground for Mr Eden's call in 1940 to join the Home Guard. Veiled orders from the squire, the parson, the big landowner to volunteer were, in Shropshire, quickly obeyed.

Throughout Shropshire there were numberless cases of retired senior Regular, or Territorial, Army Officers joining up. They all came in with the last rank they held before retirement from the Regulars, or Territorials, but nevertheless all willingly served in any capacity. In several cases a retired colonel might command a company, another might be adjutant, while the battalion commander who had first raised the unit, had retired perhaps as a captain. The author of this book recalls when a junior captain in 1928 in India, his brigade commander on his eminence. In 1941 when commanding a battalion and lecturing Home Guard officers, he saw this same brigadier, now a Home Guard company commander, sitting well back in the hall among the other junior officers. After the lecture, contact was made, each calling the other 'sir'. (In one unit a retired lieutenant-general had joined the Home Guard at Mr Eden's call. He insisted on wearing in the ranks the full insignia of his rank, his red-tabs and, of course, his rows of medal ribbons. He refused any promotion but accepted the unanimous request of all the twelve men in his section to take command. Eventually he was ordered by Command Headquarters not to wear his embellishments and to adopt a dress more suited to a section commander – usually a lance corporal. In what other army would Regular Officers subordinate in such a way their rank and prestige for the good of their country?)

Those units, however, from country districts, lacking the opportunities available to their big-town brothers were not to be outdone in ingenuity or aggression. Sporting guns were an obvious weapon for the farmers' sons, while pitch-forks in the absence of bayonets were, in the early days, very evident. Jam-tin bombs were improvized, using gunpowder from shot-gun cartridges when the farmer had a good supply. In one instance an empty drain pipe was fitted to a rough wooden stand, half-filled with pebbles, and a wooden plunger fitted at the bottom. It was fired by a strong spring, rather on the bow-and-arrow principle, which gave the plunger a violent blow upwards and this, in turn, shot out the pebbles. Naturally its range was very limited, twenty yards being extreme, and, apart from firing in ambush behind a hedge at a crossroads, was not very effective. Its chief value was psychological, the men inventing it, making it, practising with it, all feeling it was their contribution to the nation's defence.

Shropshire raised eleven battalions and, in 1943, had 766 officers of almost all ages, certainly of all grades, and 16,800 men in the ranks.

Some battalions covered enormous areas, very thinly spread, and in the far western parts of the county, up against the Welsh hills, parades were difficult to organize, reach or supervise. But the extreme toughness of the men's constitutions, owing to their outdoor occupations, coupled with their intense local *esprit de corps*, amply made up for any deficiencies in their training.

WARWICKSHIRE

UNLIKE the counties of Worcestershire, Herefordshire and Shropshire, Warwickshire has very few prehistoric remains of any account. There are but eight hillforts, only one of which, Corley, four miles north west of Coventry, has been excavated. It dates from about 300 BC and seems to have been but a temporary refuge from marauders and hardly of a military intent or interest. Likewise the Romans, excepting for three great roads they drove through the area, made little impact on the county and it was not until just before the Conquest that Warwick Castle was built. This event may fairly be stated to be the beginning of the county's history.

Until this time Warwickshire was a densely wooded, sparsely populated area. Until the fifth century the people were primitive, wild animals roamed the area. There were no towns, of course, and villages were merely collections of huts in clearings in the woods. The wooded areas were of great density, and many of the existing woods today are the remains of the great forests. Doubtless the oak trees in the Forest of Arden today are descendants of the originals. These forests of Arden and Wyre were impassable barriers to the Romans, Normans, Saxon, and Danish invaders, who lapped round their edges, unable or unwilling to penetrate. Two characteristics spring today from this original heavily wooded locale, the extreme parochialism and lack of sophistication of the villagers, and the distinctive title of 'leafy Warwickshire'.

The Dark Ages in Warwickshire only came to an end in the eleventh century during the reign of Edward the Confessor, when the only prominent persons in the county were Leofric, Earl of March, and his wife, Godiva. But the story of the lady's famous and romantic ride, naked through the large village of Coventry, is but a legend dating from the thirteenth century.

Warwickshire played one brief, but not unimportant part in the wars of the barons. Simon de Montfort, the 'great parliamentarian' and brother-in-law of King Henry III, was asked by the great barons to lead them in war against the king whose persistent and deliberate erosion of the terms of Magna Carta signed by his father, King John, was infuriating them. Simon led them to victory at the battle of Lewes in 1264, defeating the royal army and capturing King Henry and his eldest son, Prince Edward. He became virtually dictator of England, and set up the principle of popular representation in a 'parlement'. As a result of his democratic ideas, two persons from every shire and two from every town were elected to join the Great Council in London. (After some years these elected members separated from the hereditary members, sitting in their own House, becoming the House of Commons of today.)

But in May 1265, Prince Edward escaped from Simon de Montfort's captivity and at once collected an army to fight Simon and challenge his usurpation of supreme authority. His other equally congenial task was to release his father, the king, from Simon's custody. On 31 July he and his army were at Worcester.

By late July Simon de Montfort had been campaigning in Wales, mostly showing the flag, quelling uprisings against his authority, and making a triumphal progress. In his camp was, of course, the king, still a prisoner of war. On 29 July, hearing that Prince Edward was at Worcester with his newly-raised army, Simon marched through Hereford, eastward, to meet him. At the same time he directed his son, Simon the younger, who had a scratch force at Kenilworth, to await the convoy of supplies coming up from London, and then to march to meet him near Evesham. Incidentally, this mention of a supply convoy is one of the very rare occasions that such an essential part of military operations appears in medieval records.

Prince Edward now had a difficult choice before

him. He knew of young Simon's situation at Kenilworth, only thirty-four miles away, with an army of doubtful size, quality and leader. But his great objective was the elder Simon. It was far more important to defeat him and thereby release the king, and Simon senior was only twenty-seven miles away. Edward knew that the latter was probably numerically not so strong as the son, but the father, the victor of Lewes, was in command and his power, prestige and better trained force, made him the more formidable. Edward chose to settle first with the son.

THE BATTLE OF KENILWORTH

On the night of 31 July/1 August Prince Edward marched all night to Kenilworth, crossing into Warwickshire near Alcester. He then passed through Henley-in-Arden, and Warwick, reaching Kenilworth about 7 a.m.

The town, small and of only about one thousand people in 1265, centred round the great castle, a magnificent edifice already a hundred years old. (It had been granted to Simon de Montfort by King Henry, and it was here that the king and Prince Edward had first been brought after their capture at Lewes in 1264. Its first owner had been one Geoffrey de Clinton, treasurer to King Henry I – son of the Conqueror. Today the road from Kenilworth to Coleshill running north from Castle Green is called Clinton Lane. Edward had escaped when Simon moved into the West Country with the king as his prisoner, and Kenilworth was regarded as the military headquarters of the barons in rebellion against the monarch.

Young Simon was not a good soldier, and had he not been his father's son, would have made little mark in the world. His army was billeted in the houses by the castle, overlooking the green. He took no steps to protect his force from surprise, there were no outposts, no sentries, and his army had in the past few days spent many hours bathing in the river Finham, a sizeable stream or brook, a

Old houses on Castle Green, Kenilworth. Prince Edward's first attack was on the town where many of the troops of the younger Simon de Montfort were slaughtered in their beds in this area.

Kenilworth Castle: the present bridge over the ford where de Montfort's troops bathed before the battle, and the triumphant men of Prince Edward bathed following their victory.

tributary of the River Avon. It flows round the west and south sides of the castle, which stands on a slight rise, and acted as a not very effective moat on three sides. The motorist, driving from Warwick north to Coleshill and Lichfield, used to pass through a considerable ford on leaving the modern town of Kenilworth, and on approaching Castle Green. This ford has now been bridged but the stream is the same Finham brook where young Simon's soldiers bathed.

Edward's army, despite its all-night march, attacked the town and houses at once. Simon's men

Kenilworth Castle in 1620. Although many years later than Prince Edward's assault, this drawing shows the vast sheet of water (now drained) which surrounded the castle and shows why Prince Edward did not attack the castle itself at the first battle. When he returned to reduce the castle after Evesham, he did so by encirclement and siege which took him six months.

were taken by surprise, and many were killed asleep in their beds. Some escaped across the stream to the east, including young Simon himself. The majority of the fighting, such as it was, occurred astride the road up from Warwick, at the ford, and on the green. The de Montfort army was utterly defeated and dispersed.

Much booty was taken, including the newly arrived supply column with many horses and banners. The horses were invaluable for the transport of Edward's tired men, and the banners were to be put to use later.

Edward made no attempt to capture Kenilworth Castle, having no engines of war, and allowed his men a day's bathing and rest after their strenuous night. The next night, however, being satisfied that young Simon's army had been destroyed, he marched his force back to Worcester, thus covering the staggering total of over sixty miles in forty-eight hours over roads barely worth the name, and his men in footgear, at best, made of felt. But Prince Edward was a great man, and a great leader, and his men would follow him anywhere. He was to become King Edward I, one of England's great kings.

The banners he captured were put to good use on the morning of 4 August. On the 3rd Edward marched south to near Evesham to meet Simon senior's army now approaching from Pershore. Taking up a position along the high ground a mile and a half north of Evesham he raised the captured banners. A watchman on the tower of Evesham church, a local barber, saw them and reported to Simon who understandably assumed them to indicate his son's force from Kenilworth. It was some time before he realized that these banners were now carried by his enemy.

This delay by Simon de Montfort in advancing from Evesham not only enabled Edward to perfect his line and arrangements, but also gave his men a little more respite. They had now spent three nights out of the past four on their feet, and were very tired. The battle of Kenilworth, little known in history, and the captured banners, had indeed a minor effect on the battle of Evesham.

After the great battle Prince Edward returned to

Kenilworth to besiege the castle. His only siege weapons being encirclement and thus starvation, the operation took six months. It ended in indescribable suffering for the beleagured garrison which only capitulated under the compulsion of disease, famine and the death of many men.

Tragically it was at Kenilworth Castle that Edward II, the great Edward's son, heard the news of his dethronement and from there he was taken to Berkeley Castle and his murder.

Warwick Castle

Warwick Castle, the earliest parts of which were built before the Conquest, and about the time of Lady Godiva's legendary ride through Coventry, is a magnificent and enormous edifice. The family of the Earl of March, Lady Godiva's husband, held it until 1080 when they were dispossessed by King William I in favour of the first Earl of Warwick, a Norman.

Warwick Castle is one of the last of the great medieval fortresses to remain inhabited today. The first Norman knight was succeeded as owner by Simon de Montfort. Next came the Beauchamp family and then the Nevilles, of whom the most famous was the 'King Maker'. Despite the tre-

Above Helmet of Oliver Cromwell in the armour collection at Warwick Castle.

Below Warwick Castle. One of the last great medieval fortresses to remain inhabited today. Immensely strong, it has had an uneventful history.

mendous part Neville played in the Wars of the Roses, his castle was not attacked or molested in any way. Indeed for such a great fortress in the centre of England, of such importance as the home of such a powerful family, it is surprising how uneventful its history has been.

It is, and was, immensely strong, standing on a high mound in a crook of the River Avon which runs along its south walls. A wide and deep moat defends the three remaining sides. It is 300 yards long, and has four great towers, one of which, Guy's Tower, has walls ten feet thick. There has been much restoration, many additions and repairs through the centuries; and, had anything of any military or political importance occurred here, Warwick Castle would be one of the greatest of the country's monuments. Its magnificent collection of pictures, armour and furniture does not concern this book, except, from a military point of interest, a sword over five feet long, made in 1280, designed for two hands, and one of the targes or shields which Bonny Prince Charlie gave as trophies to his supporters in the 1745 rebellion. Only thirteen were made and this one is the last to survive.

Henry Tudor lands at Milford Haven

Warwickshire's part in the Wars of the Roses was only minor, consisting of a meeting between Henry Tudor, soon to be Henry VII and two members of the Stanley family two days before the Battle of Bosworth in Leicestershire. Bosworth was one of the decisive battles of English history, in that it brought to an end the thirty years' Wars of the Roses, saw the final overthrow of the House of York and the firm establishment of the House of Tudor on the throne, a dynasty that was to reign for 118 years, and to include Henry VIII and Queen Elizabeth I.

Henry Tudor had landed from France at the request of some of the leading English politicians. They were disgusted with the monarchy of Richard III – a disgust sharpened by the fate of the little princes in the Tower – and although supporters of the Yorkist king many thought a Lancastrian could do no worse, and might do better.

Henry landed at Milford Haven and marched through Wales, where his family name of Tudor brought him many recruits, reaching Tamworth on the borders of Staffordshire and Warwickshire. Crossing into Warwickshire he marched down to Atherstone where he met the two brothers Stanley and slept the night at the Three Tuns inn.

Lord Stanley, the elder brother, was in a difficult position. On the one hand he was stepfather to Henry Tudor, whose ascent of the throne he strongly supported, and, pleading illness, he had already refused to march with his large numbers of family retainers to join King Richard's army at Nottingham. On the other hand his eldest son, Lord Strange, was at Richard's court, and the king kept him as hostage to answer, doubtless with his life, for his father's loyalty. The younger Stanley brother, Sir William, had already been declared a traitor by the king and he knew that his only future lay with Henry.

BOSWORTH FIELD

A secret conference on the night of 20/21 August was held at Atherstone between Henry and the two Stanleys. Henry believed that the brothers would come in on his side when he met Richard's army, but despite their assurances, remained apprehensive. Next day he marched out of Atherstone, and Warwickshire, to meet and defeat Richard at Bosworth Field.

The preliminaries to the battle presented a situation much like the kick-off at a modern football match. The two armies, Yorkist and Tudor, stood facing each other, waiting, so to speak, for the referee's whistle. On the two touchlines stood the respective armies of the Stanleys, waiting to see who would score first, before they joined in.

The clash came about 7 a.m. on the 22nd, and after considerable exchanges lasting some hours Henry appeared to be getting the upper hand. The two opportunists on the flanks advanced, Sir William the proclaimed traitor, coming in on Richard's right rear, while Lord Stanley advanced around Richard's left. Their intervention was decisive, Richard was killed, and the Yorkist army disintegrated.

Had the two Stanleys not intervened it was possible, perhaps probable, that Richard with his superior generalship might have won. The Yorkists would have reigned supreme. Richard, having no children by his marriage to Anne widow of the Prince of Wales, would have been succeeded by his brother, William, a totally unknown figure. There is little doubt that Henry's arguments and his powers of persuasion at the Atherstone conference won over both Stanleys, thus securing the Tudor victory. The importance of the Warwickshire conference in English monarchical history can hardly be exaggerated.

For the next 157 years no military events occurred in Warwickshire. During this long period no battle was fought on English soil, no English king took the field at the head of the army. All through the Tudor era there was peace in England.

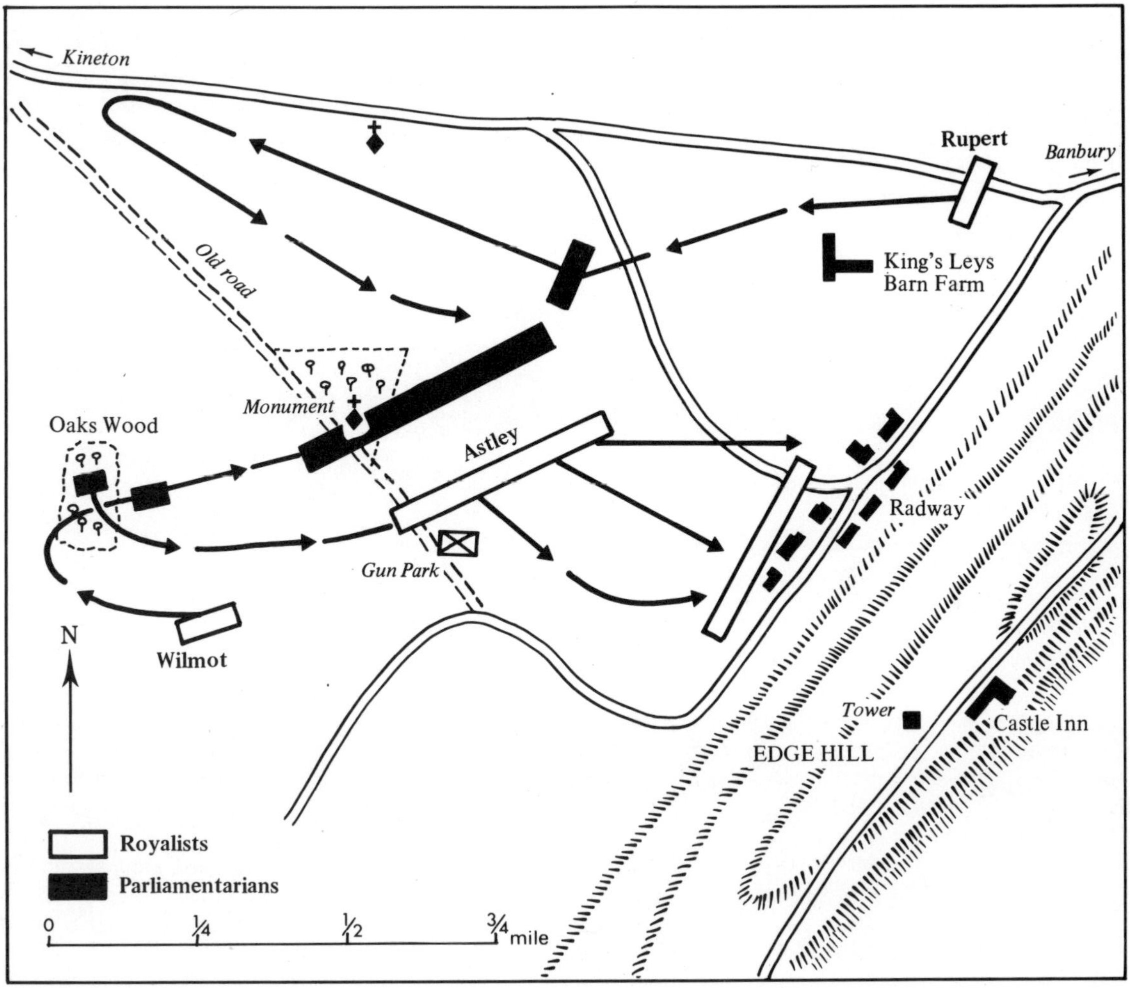

Battle of Edgehill

BATTLE OF EDGEHILL

The Battle of Edgehill, Warwickshire, in 1642 was the opening engagement of the Civil War.

The Tudors were succeeded by the four Stuarts, three of whom brought trouble and strife to the country. The first Stuart, James I, had been harsh, arrogant and tactless. He told Parliament that, as it was blasphemy to dispute what God might do, so it was sedition to dispute what God's lieutenant upon earth might do. From the day of that speech in 1611 Parliament was arrayed against the king. On one occasion the Commons suggested a suitable line on a foreign affair. They were told by James that it was not their business. In their Journal, they entered a protest, passed in the House, adding that they were free to discuss any topic. James sent for the Journal and tore out that page.

James I was an able and intelligent man, but it was a pity that he did not recognize the dawning consciousness of Englishmen to their own rights, abilities, and reasonable desire to participate in their country's affairs.

His son, Charles I, although a less able man than his father, was more stubborn, rigid and bigoted. In religious matters in particular, partly due to the influence of his Roman Catholic wife, he was quite immovable in his attitudes in support of everything Catholic and against anything giving encouragement to Protestants. The queen actively intrigued with foreign powers, and worst of all held the most extreme political opinions as to the king's authority, the royal supremacy, and the wickedness of all who opposed it.

On Charles's succession he found the Treasury in low water. He needed money to equip a fleet to attack Spain and to prosecute the long-drawn-out war with Scotland. Parliament would not grant the funds, and Charles threatened to take taxation entirely into his own hands and levy a forced loan.

Charles had already dissolved two parliaments, but now called together a third one. Its first act was to pass the Petition of Right, the two most important clauses being that the taxation of the people except by consent of Parliament was illegal, and that arbitrary imprisonment without cause was also outside the law.

Finally the king went down to the House of Commons with four hundred soldiers to arrest five leading members on a charge of treason. The five members having been warned of such action on the part of the king were deliberately absent. But the damage was done. The members greatly resented the personal intrusion of the monarch into their Chamber, regarding it as a scandalous breach of privilege, and on his departure he was hooted out of the building with cries of 'Privilege, privilege'.

Both sides made preparations for war in the next seven months and in August 1642 Charles raised his standard at Nottingham Castle. The great Civil War had begun: it was to last seven years.

The English people were split into two camps; one patriotic, adhering to the King, loyal to the principle of monarchy, the divine right of kings, the Lord's annointed. The other, also patriotic, loyal to their country and its welfare, believed in the sovereignty of the people, believed in the seventeenth century.

The king's men, the Cavaliers, drew their strength from the nobility, the landed gentry and their retainers, and the small townsmen. They were strong in cavalry, with an eye for the tactical use of ground; the men were easily led as the men in the county regiments have always been. They were tough, used to exposure, not over-intelligent and followed the king as their man, the man they loved. He was a 'gentleman'.

The Roundheads were largely city men, narrow in outlook, quick, intelligent and capable, easy to teach, quick to learn, and by their intelligence convinced of the righteousness of their cause – democracy, and self-expression.

On Charles's declaration at Nottingham of war against his Parliament, the Earl of Essex marched from London with a not very good Parliamentary army to meet him. Charles made for Worcester, and Essex pushed on there to catch him. But bad Parliamentary staff-work lost the Royalist army, and Charles went east and made for his capital. Essex, hearing of this move several hours later, turned and followed.

Charles now had two courses to choose from – turn round and face his pursuing enemy, or continue his march on London.

One of Charles's great assets was his nephew Prince Rupert of the Rhine, a born cavalry leader, aged twenty-three, and utterly devoted to his uncle's cause. He urgently advocated standing and fighting, believing that his cavalry could easily deal with the Parliamentary townsmen while the better trained and experienced Royalist infantry could withstand any Roundhead advance. Charles agreed and halted his army on the ridge of Edgehill and below it in the little village of Radway.

Opposite above Charlecote showing at left (the parkland with isolated trees) where Prince Rupert's troops camped before Edgehill.
Below Charles I with Prince Rupert issuing the order of battle before Edgehill. From the painting by Charles Landseer.
Overleaf The scene of the Battle of Edgehill, 1642.

Edgehill is a long ridge, 600 feet high, between Banbury and Warwick. On the morning of 23 October Charles, from a large watchtower on the ridge close to the Castle Inn, saw Essex moving slowly south-east from the village of Kineton. At once he moved the balance of his army down the hill, and there with the remainder of his army took up a position about a mile north-west of Radway.

The line had infantry in the centre, with cavalry on either flank, Prince Rupert commanding the right wing. The centre infantry group was a thousand yards to the west of the village of Radway. Charles's 13,000 men must have presented a formidable sight to Essex's army of 12,000 as it moved out of Kineton to form about a mile short of the Royalists. The central infantry of each army exactly matched each other. The Parliamentarian right flank rested on the southern edge of a wood, the Oaks.

At 11 a.m. the Royalist cavalry on both flanks attacked. Rupert moved astride the Knowle End – Kineton Road – his left passing within a few yards of the farm known as King's Leys Barn.

Meanwhile the Royalist infantry in the centre advanced for half a mile. As the action started, old Astley, its commander, made his famous prayer – 'O Lord, Thou knowest how busy I shall be this day. If I forget Thee, do Thou not forget me. March on, boys.' They pushed back some Roundhead groups slightly but the latter resisted and a stalemate developed. This so far unimportant little action was witnessed at very close quarters by two little boys, aged eleven and nine, the future Charles II and his brother James II. Their truancy from the Royal headquarters was discovered and they were hurried back to the safety of Edgehill.

At the same time as Rupert led his cavalry forward Lord Wilmot led the Royal cavalry on the left. Making a big sweep round to the west he drove away Fielden's Parliamentary regiment out beyond the Oaks, and then turned inwards to attack the Parliamentary right wing. But in the wood were two enemy cavalry regiments. One engaged Wilmot, while the other came out of the wood and passing round his comrade's right flank, charged the Royalist infantry centre. This he decimated and reached the Royalist gun-park in the wood. (The site of this Royalist gun-park of 1642 is today occupied by an Army Ordnance depot, storing gun ammunition. Access by the general public is not permitted.)

Another Parliamentarian cavalry attack supported by the infantry was mounted and, at first, the Royalist's left flank was pushed back almost into Radway, but their line held.

Now Rupert intervened. Returning from his charge he found on the battlefield two exhausted armies. Although the Parliamentarians needed perhaps only one more 'push of pike' for victory, the sight of Rupert's cavalry entering the battlefield deterred them. The king's army still held. A few guns not over-run opened fire, and the Parliamentarians paused. Firing died away and in the night they withdrew. That night Charles slept in King's Leys Barn farm. In the last Parliamentary cavalry attack which pushed the Royalists back towards Radway was a troop commanded by a Captain Oliver Cromwell.

Many historians classify Edgehill as a drawn battle, neither side having a resounding win. Edgehill was not a draw. The avowed intention of Essex was to bring the king's army to battle, to defeat it and to prevent the king marching on London. He failed. In his attack he was repulsed by the Royalists who held their ground, and unquestionably Essex was defeated. Equally the king won. He took up a defensive position which he held all day, and by repulsing Essex who withdrew to Warwick, was able after giving his men a day's rest to resume his march on London, his original intention.

To see the battlefield is difficult, because of Ministry of Defence restrictions. However, take the A41, Banbury-Warwick road. Turn left along B4086. Thence the road passes on its left within five hundred yards of King's Leys Barn farm, now only a heap of rubble. Return through Kineton along the third-class road to Radway. A mile and a quarter along this road is the Oaks, five hundred yards away. It is impossible to reach the Oaks owing to MOD restrictions. The monument to the battle is on this road, on the edge of Grave Ground. In this wood, lying between Thistle Farm and Battle Farm, are the graves of five hundred men from both sides, killed in the battle.

An excellent view of the whole battlefield can be obtained from the Castle Inn at Ratley Grange, on Edgehill itself. Its imposing tower, from which King Charles made his first reconnaissance and from which he later moved down on to the battlefield, provides an excellent viewpoint and more will be gained with field glasses and a map from this

Opposite An excellent view of the whole battlefield can be seen from the tower at the Castle Inn, Ratley Grange, on Edgehill. From this tower Charles I made his first reconnaissance and later moved down into the battle.

point than from any attempts to make a closer visit.

One little relic of the Civil War remains in Warwickshire. Two nights before the battle of Edgehill, Prince Rupert's cavalry encamped for the night in the park of Charlecote, the great Elizabethan home of the Lucys. They actually tethered their horses and slept in the Great Meadow, Rupert sleeping in the house. After the Civil War the name of Great Meadow was changed to Camp Ground, the name it bears today.

WARWICKSHIRE'S MILITARY UNITS

It will be recalled from the chapters on Worcestershire and Shropshire how King Charles II and his government realized the absolute necessity of replacing Cromwell's New Model Army. This army had been disbanded in 1660 some years after the battle of Worcester in 1651, and England stood naked on land with no military forces whatever, and the Navy as its only protective force. Consequently new regular regiments were raised, to be a standing army, paid by Parliament under whose control they were to remain.

The first five regiments to be raised came from the Lowlands of Scotland, Surrey, Kent, Lancashire, and Northumberland, a wide area. The 5th Fusiliers were formed in 1674, thirteen years after the oldest, the 2nd Foot, The Queen's.

In 1688 many members of Parliament, and some of the leading members of the aristocracy had become so disgusted with the bigoted and dictatorial methods of James II that they invited Prince William of Orange, grandson of Charles I, and his wife Mary, daughter of King James, to come over from the Netherlands and become joint sovereigns. William landed at Torbay, James ran away to France never to set foot in England again, and William, later joined by his wife, Princess Mary, reigned as William and Mary, joint monarchs, but with all power, leadership and influence in William's hands, willingly surrendered by Mary.

The 6th (Royal Warwicks)

William brought with him two regiments, which were quickly absorbed into The Line, becoming the 6th (Royal Warwicks) and 7th (Royal Fusiliers).

Like all regiments of the Line the title of the Royal Warwicks was changed through the years several times. The greatest change came in 1963 when it became the Royal Warwickshire Fusiliers, the word 'Regiment' being dropped. This (to a regiment) sweeping change became necessary when all the regiments of infantry were grouped into administrative brigades or 'large' regiments, and the three existing Fusilier regiments, the Northumberland, Royal, and Lancashire needed a fourth to become a large regiment in the new set-up. The Royal Warwicks were chosen.

Since its formation in 1688 the Royal Warwicks had fought in many of the Empire's famous engagements. The Boyne, the Peninsular War with several engagements, Aden, India, the Kaffir wars, the Indian Mutiny, Khartoum, and South Africa all saw the regiment. It missed both Waterloo and the Crimea being on Indian and South African garrison duty at the time. But one incident not connected with war must be recounted.

In January 1852 the troopship *Birkenhead* sailed from Cork with reinforcements for regiments at the Cape. There were six hundred and thirty-eight men on board, one officer – Lieutenant Metford – one sergeant and fifty-eight men of the Royal Warwicks being the largest of the drafts. When the ship called at the Cape, Lieut Metford's wife was left behind through sickness and the *Birkenhead* sailed on for Algoa Bay. In the middle of the night of 25 February the ship struck a rock and quickly settled. It was evident that she must break up and boats were lowered to get the women and children ashore. The detachments of all regiments on board were lined up and the OC Troops told the officers that discipline and silence were never more necessary if even a few men were to be saved in the last remaining boats. As the ship was about to sink the captain told all men who could swim to jump overboard, but the OC Troops forbade it believing that the boats would thus become overloaded and the lives of the women and children endangered. Only three men obeyed the captain while the vast majority took their turn to fill the remaining boats. Eventually only one hundred and ninety-three were saved, six hundred and thirty-eight were drowned, Lieutenant

The Warwickshire Regiment (6th Foot) – the Royal Warwicks – at Omdurman near Khartoum in 1898, an engagement in which Sir Winston Churchill took part in the charge of the 21st Lancers.

Metford and forty-seven men of the Royal Warwicks among them.

The bravery, discipline, and self-sacrifice of the men lost created a great wave of sympathy and admiration not only in the Army and England, but throughout the world. Indeed the King of Prussia ordered a record of this devotion to duty to be read out at the head of every regiment in his Army.

World War I

In August 1914, on the outbreak of the First World War the 1st Battalion of the Royal Warwicks was stationed at Shorncliffe as part of the 4th Division. This division was kept back from the original British Expeditionary Force to protect the east and south coasts of England from a possible German invasion, but it was soon realized that such an invasion was impossible and the 4th Division crossed to France eight days after the original four divisions. Consequently the division missed the Battle of Mons and only came into action for the first time at Le Cateau. Here it was on the extreme left and outer flank of the whole Allied Force.

At dawn on 26 August, the right forward battalion of the left-hand brigade of the 4th Division, The Kings Own, was caught in mass on a forward slope by German machine-guns and artillery. It suffered very heavily, eighty-three men, including the CO, being killed and a total of four hundred men becoming casualties. The Second-in-Command withdrew the battalion back to behind the ridge close at hand – which it should never have left – and the Royal Warwicks from the reserve brigade came forward to fill the gap, the Regiment's first action in the war. It, too, suffered heavily. However, the battalions on their right and left, the Hampshires and the Lancashire Fusiliers, now opened fire on the advancing German infantry and held them. All day attempts were made by the enemy to get forward, but to no avail and the British line held firm until the evening. As dusk fell the Corps Commander, Sir Horace Smith-Dorien, gave the order for a general withdrawal all along the line and by 10 p.m. the great Retreat from Mons was continued, to last eleven days, and for the troops to cover in some cases one hundred and fifty miles.

One of the platoon commanders in the Royal Warwicks that day, a young officer twenty-six years old and with six years service, was Lieutenant Bernard Montgomery, later Field Marshal Viscount Montgomery of Alamein. In the 1st Division, also in the great Retreat from Mons, on an almost parallel road fifteen miles to the east, marched another platoon commander in the Irish Guards, Lieutenant Harold Alexander, later to be Field Marshal Earl Alexander of Tunis. The Royal Warwicks remained in the famous 4th Division throughout the War, taking its full part in all the major engagements.

The 2nd Battalion was in Malta when the war broke out, and being brought home to England formed part of the equally famous 7th Division which was part of the rescue Corps sent out to Italy after the Italian disaster at Caporetto in November 1917.

The 143 Brigade on the Somme

The Royal Warwickshire Regiment raised altogether ten battalions for Kitchener's Army in 1914 and 1915 as well as eight second-line Territorial battalions. But it is of the 1st line Territorial battalions, units existing in August 1914 and which had already been in existence as volunteers for many years, which we must consider more fully.

Of the three British armies existing or about to exist in the autumn of 1914, the Regulars, Territorials and Kitchener's Army, it was the Territorials who felt most acutely the harsh transition from peace-time life to active service.

More than half of all Regulars were, in 1914, on foreign service, mostly in India and Egypt, where the lack of home comforts and the extreme heat, dust and disease barely worried the young bachelor soldiers with an average age of twenty-four. The Retreat from Mons and the mud of Ypres were all part of their job, liabilities they accepted on voluntary enlistment in peace time. The men of Kitchener's Army similarly accepted the same probabilities but were not called on to experience mud, the extreme discomfort of the trenches, danger, or real fatigue for a year after enlistment.

The Territorial soldiers, however, had in many cases found themselves in the trenches at the First Battle of Ypres in November, 1914, only four months after being embodied. Several Territorial battalions, mostly from London, had to be sent into action as complete units, long before they were fit to do so, suffering heavy casualties through inexperience.

On the declaration of war, the fourteen Territorial divisions were embodied, retaining their identity, both military and geographical, throughout the war. All divisional, brigade and unit organization had existed in peacetime, ever since Haldane constituted the Territorial Army from the Volunteers in

1908. Always stationed in the same town or district in peace-time, individuals knowing each other in civil life, in business, clubs and pubs, the officers as local as the men, a superb unit *esprit de corps* existed, at least the equal to that of Regular battalions. Unlike the Regular Army, games and

Officers of the 2nd Royal Warwickshires in the Ypres salient, 1915. A unique photograph taken before the ban on press photographers was lifted.

sport played little part in their military life or in their inter-unit rivalry.

Prior to August 1914 a considerable proportion of both officers and men were compelled by their civilian employers to count the annual fortnight in camp as their holiday. Other, more generous employers would perhaps give one week's extra holiday as well as two weeks' time off for 'camp'. The Territorials prior to August 1914, were typical of the national character as it was then. They were unselfish, patriotic, co-operative and adventurous.

The weakness of all the Territorial battalions was thought to lie in discipline and training. In peace time the former was easily maintained in the annual two weeks' camp and weekly drill nights at the local drill-hall by a most willing and co-operative obedience. But it was thought probable, although by no means certain, that if war came this almost self-imposed discipline would not stand its only test, the ability to stand firm when times are bad and the enemy looks like being successful. In the event it greatly exceeded the wildest hopes.

Training, both individual and collective tactical, was very uneven. Some officers, good at platoon and company tactics, were almost ignorant of weapon training. Others excellent at drill could barely read a map. It was thought in August 1914 that at least six months would be needed to bring discipline and training up to the necessary standard. Little or no time need be spent on organization of the units. It was all in existence.

The fourteen Territorial Divisions and Brigades were not numbered prior to August, 1914, and were known only by their locality or parent regiments. This was an additional aid to *esprit de corps*, especially in those brigades that had four battalions of the same regiment in them.

The Royal Warwicks had four of these excellent units: the 5th and 6th from the centre of Birmingham; the 7th from Coventry; the 8th from Aston with outlying companies. They formed a brigade, the 143rd in the 48th South Midland Territorial Division. This brigade was very good, and was one of several in the Territorial Army to have all its battalions from one regiment; the 5th, 6th and 7th Royal Warwicks were entirely composed of city men from the suburbs of Birmingham and Coventry, living in town conditions, and having an urban outlook. In the 8th, however, three companies came from small outlying towns and the men had a different psychological outlook from those from the big cities.

The 143 Brigade's greatest exploit during its four years' service in France, Flanders and Italy was probably in August 1916 in the Battle of the Somme. The 143 Brigade, on the right of the 48th Division, attacked northward from near Ovillers to outflank Thiepval. Those men alive today who were in the Battle of the Somme will remember Thiepval on its hill and how it defied capture from the opening day of the battle, 1 July, until 26 September, nearly three months later. The 5th and 6th Royal Warwicks led the brigade, and advancing on a one-thousand-yard frontage, penetrated and captured the enemy's lines to a depth of five hundred yards. This capture of five hundred thousand square yards seems trivial enough today, but in trench warfare and against such a redoubtable enemy it was brilliant.

The right-hand battalion, the 5th, captured one fortified post from which emerged six officers and two hundred and forty-four men, all unwounded. One of the officers in the 6th, Captain Crockford, a first-class shot, got behind an enemy sandbag barricade and while his men lobbed Mills bombs over his head, he fired one man's rifle continuously and put an enemy machine-gun team entirely out of action. Another machine-gun, temporarily deserted by its German team, was isolated by Corporal Haseler who jumped into the enemy trench and from behind a traverse, or what was left of it, shot every enemy soldier who tried to reach the gun. Captain Crockford was awarded the MC and Corporal Haseler the DCM. The total casualties in the brigade from all causes were less than three hundred.

The last Austrian offensive

This Warwickshire brigade, always one of the most reliable in the army, went out to the Italian front after Passchendaele in 1917 with the 48th Division. Here on the Asiago Plateau it was the left-hand brigade of the British Corps of three divisions, and took, with its neighbour the 145 brigade, the full force of the last great Austrian attack on 15 July 1918. The 145 brigade had rough handling and the 5th Gloucesters and 4th Oxford and Bucks were pushed back. (The forward Company Commander in the 5th Gloucesters had a twenty-eight-day leave warrant in his pocket for next day when he was captured.) The 5th Royal Warwicks were holding the 143 brigade's front, and were also pushed back. Battalion Headquarters was nearly surrounded, the CO was killed but the RSM formed a strong-point with signallers, cooks, batmen, etc., and held out

The Royal Warwickshires coming out of the battle of the Somme in 1916 at Beaumont Hamel. The troops in the picture are probably the 1st Battalion and not one of the two Territorial Batteries that took part.

until darkness. Next day at dawn the 6th and 7th counter-attacked, relieving the beleagured sergeant major's post, and entirely restoring the line to its original trenches.

After the collapse of this great Austrian offensive the summer months passed uneventfully on the Asiago Plateau. Life in the line was very quiet indeed, the weather could not have been better and the troops preferred to stay in the trenches with their peaceful atmosphere, regular and good rations and absence of parades, rather than march for three days down to the plains, where the temperature was torrid, often reaching 95°, much 'cleaning up' and then a three-day march back to the Plateau, up hill all the way.

Life in the line in July and August was enlivened by night raids and the 143 became very keen. On the left of the British front, and opposite the Royal Warwicks Territorials, 'no man's land' was often a mile wide and the raiding parties could and did range at will looking for, but rarely finding, any Austrians. One raid by three companies of the 5th Battalion was led by the CO, Lt. Col. Gell, while another by the 6th was under the 2nd-in-Command, Major Fox. One raid, perhaps the best known, although on a smaller scale, was highly successful, carried out by the 8th Royal Warwicks. One platoon with blackened faces and hands, in steel helmets, and carrying only entrenching-tool handles, was formed into two equal parties four hundred yards apart, just behind the British front line. Precisely at 2 a.m. the two parties, led respectively by their officer and sergeant, passed through the wire and moved due north by compass bearing. Crossing the enemy front-line trench the officer with the left-hand party blew his whistle and both parties turned inwards towards each other. When they met, another blast of the whistle told the men to turn in again – now towards home. Driving any enemy encountered before them, they shepherded one hundred and twenty-five unwounded Austrians back to the British lines, and there was not one Royal Warwick casualty.

This 143 Brigade Commander was the outstanding soldier in this remarkable brigade. Captain Sladen had been the Regular Territorial Adjutant of the 8th Royal Warwicks for a year in August 1914. In 1915, as a result of casualties he was sent to command the 5th Battalion, remaining as CO until late 1916 when he was promoted to the command of the 143 Brigade, where he remained until after the Armistice in November 1918. Thus he not only remained in the same brigade throughout the war but was also one of the few regular officers in the army who, a captain in 1914, was to reach the rank of Brigadier-General, in Sladen's case, within three years.

World War II

The story of the Royal Warwickshire Regiment in World War II is similar to other regiments, the exception being the story of the 1st Battalion.

The 2nd Battalion was at Aldershot in 1939, in the 1st Division and went out to France with the BEF. Evacuated from Dunkirk, it spent the next four years in England and then, being posted to the famous 3rd Division, was one of the earlier battalions to land in Normandy on D-Day in 1944. It fought in Europe throughout the campaign and ended, on Armistice Day, at Bremen, five hundred miles from its landing on D-Day.

Of the four Territorial battalions in the famous 143 Brigade of World War I, two had left the Regiment by 1939. The 5th was transformed into a Searchlight Battalion and became officially part of the Royal Engineers, while the 6th were transferred to the Royal Artillery as anti-aircraft gunners.

The 7th and 8th remained as infantry battalions, both going over to France in 1940, and taking part in the Dunkirk evacuation. The 7th returned to France in 1944 with the new BEF.

The 1st Battalion had an extraordinary war. Stationed in India at the outbreak, it was at once sent up to the North-West Frontier, the most dangerous and vulnerable area in the whole sub-continent, which could never be left unguarded. Here the 1st stayed until January 1942 when it was sent down to Calcutta on Internal Security duties until April 1945. Even now it had not fired a shot at the real enemy, and its only casualties had been minor ones inflicted by the tribesmen on the North-West Frontier.

Cyclist section of the 7th Battalion – Territorials from Coventry – moving up to the Belgian front in 1940.

In May 1945 it was embarked for active service, an up-river attack in Burma on Japanese-held Rangoon. However, the enemy had withdrawn and the Battalion landed unmolested in a deserted and badly-bombed city. The remainder of the Division went north but again the 1st Royal Warwicks were disappointed, being left behind in Rangoon to clear up the mess, and control the returning natives, bent on looting.

However, its chance came at last. It was sent off from Rangoon to deal with an aggressive party of the enemy left behind forty-five miles above Rangoon. One Company was employed and located, surprised, and dispersed the enemy.

By now Burma was completely dominated by the 14th Army, and movement back through India commenced. The 1st Royal Warwicks went to Bangalore where it heard the news of the atom bombs on Hiroshima and Nagasaki. The war was virtually over, and the Battalion saw no more service against an enemy. Having served overseas throughout the war, suffering only a handful of casualties, with only one Company in action once against the real enemy in the East for a brief hour, the 1st Royal Warwicks had indeed had an extraordinary war.

An enterprising Home Guard

The story of the Home Guard in Warwickshire is complicated. The county contains two great industrial cities, Birmingham and Coventry, with a total population of well over a million, and a large agricultural area with a handful of small towns. These two types of country needed very different guarding. The first called for efficient protection of extensive factories, often producing munitions of war, railway centres and big generating stations, telephone exchanges, etc. Aid to the civil power in controlling traffic in the densely populated districts after air raids, rescue work and clearing of rubble at street junctions were other equally important tasks in the two great cities. Out in the country, however,

The Royal Warwickshires with their mascot, the goat with silver-tipped horns, entering Brussels on the anniversary of the liberation of the city.

as in most rural counties, the tasks were different. Patrolling important roads, guarding crossroads, rail bridges, tunnels, approaches to aerodromes, patrolling narrow quiet country roads where suspicious strangers had been reported, were important duties. Equally important, and what the men enjoyed most, were tactical training, manoeuvres, occupation of defensive positions in case of enemy landings of organized parachutists. Musketry, Lewis-gun training, and bomb-throwing were all popular.

Altogether Warwickshire raised forty-five battalions of the Home Guard. Eight Coventry battalions operated in their own City. Sixteen were in Birmingham. The men in these two groups of battalions were enlisted from all walks of life, all trades and occupations, and formed a heterogeneous collection of individuals, similar to the battalions formed in Kitchener's Army in 1914. In addition, in Birmingham City a Public Utilities Group was formed, with two battalions composed entirely of Birmingham Corporation Transport employees, one from the Corporation gas, water and electricity supplies, and the other from the GWR and LMS staffs.

It is reported that the grouping of these public utilities workers into their own battalions proved very advantageous. Comradeship already existed before enlistment, and the concentration of each group at its own works facilitated arrangements for parades. Most of the men were accustomed to wearing uniform of some sort and often a large proportion lived in the same district. All were directly interested in defending their own place of work and livelihood.

In the memorable enemy raid on Coventry of 14 November 1940, when the heart of the city was cut out, and its cathedral virtually destroyed, the Coventry Home Guard rendered untold service. The great raid lasted eleven hours, many people being killed and injured and the damage widespread. Most of the men in the Home Guard worked through the night and in pouring rain all next day, clearing ways for traffic and pedestrians. Many were on their feet for thirty-six hours, and undoubtedly helped greatly to bring Coventry back to life again.

Other lesser raids followed, and in the period nine men were killed on duty or died of wounds received. Several of the AA batteries defending the two great cities were eventually manned entirely by the Home Guard. Two of these batteries each brought down a German aircraft, one on the battery's first night in its full and independent operational role. No wonder morale was high.

Battalions in rural or even small town districts were naturally not so lucky in finding opportunities for improvising weird weapons as those in or near large industrial towns with factories. The ingenuity of the chief engineers of those factories which made or used heavy machinery was unbelievable. The example set in the siege of Kimberley in the Boer War was followed. There, an actual field-gun on wheels that fired effectively was designed and built in the De Beers works. Known as Long Cecil, after Cecil Rhodes who was also a prisoner in Kimberley, this home-made gun was preserved and is on view outside Kimberley's Town Hall.

From these Midland factories inventions appeared frequently, all primitive, all designed by men who had no military training or knowledge. They were lethal, sometimes dangerous to their users, and when handled by the men who had actually made them, very effective. The battalions from Coventry and Birmingham were well armed.

NORTHAMPTONSHIRE

THE county, sixty miles long from north-east to south-west, yet only twenty miles wide at its centre, lies aslant the eastern midlands. This geographical situation at the heart of England has led to several military events. The battles of Naseby, Northampton, and Edgecote were fought within its borders. Through it ran two great Roman roads: Watling Street, entering the county from the south near Stony Stratford and leaving it near Rugby; and Ermine Street, the present A1, which just clips off the extreme north-east corner of the county on its way northward to Stamford. These two great roads saw much Roman military activity, legions marching along Watling Street to the garrisons of Chester, Lancaster, and the Western Frontier of England, while those on Ermine Street, moving to or from Hadrian's Wall, were a constant reminder to the peasants near the roads of the long foreign military occupation of England.

Boadicea confronts the Romans

In AD 60 the greatest revolt by the English against the Romans lasted for some months. Queen Boadicea, leader of the Icenii tribe from Norfolk and Suffolk, led a great advance south-westward. She burnt and razed Colchester so thoroughly that the site of the original settlement has never been found. She marched on to London, and Verulamium – now St Albans – both of which she burnt. Traces of this burning can still be seen in the excavations being carried out at Verulamium. She had practically no opposition in these great adventures, as Suetonius Paulinus, the Roman commander-in-chief, was away in North Wales with most of his troops.

Flushed with her success she turned north-west into the Midlands, marching up Watling Street. Here, somewhere in Northamptonshire, she met Suetonius Paulinus hurrying south to meet the revolt, and somewhere along the great road they met in battle. Suetonius had 10,000 men, tired after much marching. Boadicea had 20,000.

The exact site of the engagement is not known but there is no doubt that Suetonius went into a defensive position in 'a narrow valley, an excellent tactical position of his choosing'.

The Iceni attacked first but their frontage, restricted by the sides of the valley, was narrow, and consequently they were very closely packed. The discipline of the Roman regulars overcame the wildly enthusiastic British, who were heavily repulsed. As has happened so often in history, an early and considerable set-back was too much for the untrained English attackers and they turned and fled. The Romans advanced down the valley killing all they could find, while those British who escaped, including Boadicea herself, disappeared into the forestland of Northamptonshire in and around the area of Market Harborough, Kettering, Wellingborough, and Northampton. Understandably Boadicea's nerve was badly shaken. Not only was it quite impossible to re-assemble her army in the close country, but she was psychologically incapable of making the effort. A few days after the battle she committed suicide by poisoning herself.

There is a strong legend that she was buried in the Forest of Whittlebury although there is no evidence whatever as to even an approximate site. There are tracts of the forest surviving today in the south of the county covering a large area, and should deforestation be attempted on a large scale it is not impossible that Boadicea's grave may yet be found. All bones and clothing will long since have disintegrated but the legend claims that she was buried in her crown and with much gold jewellery. Legend always has somewhere at its base a modicum of fact. Although distorted, twisted, enlarged, the legend if traced to its source will be found to have started its long journey as a fact.

Hunsbury Hill, two miles south west of Northampton. A fortified Iron Age camp, *c.* 200 BC. Here Warwick the Kingmaker and his Yorkist army spent the night before the battle of Northampton in 1460.

Prior to the Roman occupation, Northamptonshire has little of a military story to tell. Until the Romans came the county had been merely marsh or forest and it was largely unexplored territory even for the Bronze Age people. One exception, however, is Hunsbury Hill two miles southwest of modern Northampton. On this hill Warwick the Kingmaker and his Yorkist army spent the night before the battle of Northampton in 1460. Here are the remains of a fortified camp of the Iron Age, not older than 200 BC. It was probably in use as a defensive post against the Romans in their move north-westward to the western frontier of England, but surprisingly there are no other similar prehistoric hillforts in the county nor, indeed, many Roman fortifications. The paucity of the latter implies that its marshy or tree-covered ground offered little scope for defending natives to set up resistant earthworks and clearly the Romans regarded the whole area as safely conquered and its people unlikely to revolt. Queen Boadicea, her defeat and death, brought the curtain down on Northampton's early military history. Three hundred years of Pax Romana followed.

During the Dark Ages, from AD 415 when the Romans withdrew from England until about the end of the eighth century, little of any importance happened in Northamptonshire or indeed in England. But about AD 900 raiders from across the North Sea came in and continued for 120 years. Angles, Saxons, Danes and Vikings all came over, harrying the country, burning, murdering and plundering, and the people of England lived in terror for this long period. Although the Danes tried to occupy the country permanently until Alfred the Great defeated them, forcing them back north-eastward, it was the Vikings who were the most cruel. Their method of invasion was to sail and row their boats up the rivers from the North Sea until they found a town worth sacking. Northampton on the River Nene suffered a terribly devastation in AD 1010 when it was burnt with the villages around it, everyone being killed except those who could escape into the woods.

Northampton revived by the Normans

At the time of the Norman Conquest, Northampton town was merely a collection of about three hundred houses made of mud and thatch. In 1084 William the Conqueror promoted one of his knights, Simon de Senlis, who had been wounded at Hastings, to be Earl of Northampton, with the task of building a castle and fortifying the town. The site was at a crossing of the River Nene, here flowing between considerable banks and in 1084 probably fifty yards wide – an important crossing. The defensive work was urgent, as for many years William was not sure how long he could keep the volcanic resistance of the conquered people in subjection. Large impregnable fortresses were essential and young Simon de Senlis had a great deal to do.

He built a great ring of masonry round the embryo settlement huddling against St Peter's church, then a Saxon building, but with many Norman additions. His great wall not only enclosed the existing settlement but also took in large areas of open land to accommodate troops in bivouac. These walls, often twenty feet high, followed an almost circular track and it is possible to walk their precise line today by moving along the Mounts from Abington Street (the site of the east gate), Grafton Street, St Andrews Road, Black Lion Hill, St Peter's Way, Victoria Promenade, Cheyne Walk, and York Road back to Abington Street. All traces of the wall have now disappeared, except one archway of a postern gate moved from the castle and re-erected by Black Lion Hill.

The fortified town of Northampton played a big part in the history of England in 1126 during the struggle for the throne between Stephen and Matilda. Henry I, son of the Conqueror, lost his only legitimate son in the White Ship disaster. It is useful to recall the events which led up to the great Council of Northampton. In the absence of the Salic Law, not then enacted, there could be no question that Matilda, Henry's only surviving child, was the rightful heir. But in the twelfth century it was unthinkable that a woman could be a Queen Regnant and the great nobles asked Stephen, Matilda's cousin, and a grandson of William I, to be their king. Old King Henry saw that his daughter, clearly the rightful heir, must on his death fight for her throne. To prevent a civil war likely to follow his death, he summoned to Northampton, as the centre of England, all the great nobles and leaders of the Church to a great Council. Here he told all the barons and bishops that he insisted on their swearing fealty to Matilda as the rightful heir and next monarch, before he would let them disperse. In All Saint's church, on the site of which, but much smaller, stands the present All Saint's, they all had to swear loyalty to Matilda, who sat by the High Altar and graciously acknowledged their vows individually.

Henry died nine years later and at once civil war broke out. Some of those present at the Northampton Conference kept their word and supported Matilda, others did not. A number from each side took up arms ostensibly to fight for their champion but in reality to levy war against some hated and despised rival. Old scores were wiped off, in the name of Matilda or Stephen. There was no central government, there was no monarch on the throne, anarchy ruled, and men said that during these thirteen years 'Christ and his saints slept'.

The county of Northampton appears in history again in 1290 when Eleanor of Castile, wife of Edward I, died at Harby in Lincolnshire. Edward brought her body, lying on the top of her coffin for all to see, in a gigantic funeral procession to Westminster. He erected the famous and beautiful Eleanor crosses where the coffin rested each night on its long and slow journey to London, Northamptonshire has two of them, at Geddington, near Kettering, and at Hardingstone, three miles south of Northampton. The latter cross is still in a remarkable state of preservation. It reappeared in history in 1460 in the Wars of the Roses.

St. Peter's Church, Northampton. A Saxon church centred on which Simon de Senlis, built a great ring of masonry enclosing a huddle of mud huts and camping grounds for troops, which became the town of Northampton.

Opposite This drawing made in 1805 shows details of the beautiful cross erected to the memory of Eleanor of Castile, wife of Edward I near Northampton. Engraving by J. C. Smith after G. Shepherd.

THE BATTLE OF NORTHAMPTON

A full account of the causes of the Wars of the Roses appears in the chapter on Herefordshire together with the events leading up to the battle of Mortimer's Cross in 1461. Briefly, the Yorkists won the first two battles, at St Albans in 1455 and at Blore Heath 1459. Then, unaccountably, only a month later they were beaten at Ludford, near Ludlow, when they deserted wholesale. The leading Yorkists, Richard Neville, Earl of Warwick (the Kingmaker) and Edward, Earl of March, later to be Edward IV, fled to Calais while Richard, Duke of York, crossed over to Dublin.

However, a year later in 1460 these great leaders returned to England and collected an army in London. The Lancastrians were in the Midlands, near Coventry, under the nominal command of King Henry VI, but in fact entirely dominated by the Queen, Margaret of Anjou. She moved the Lancastrian army south-eastward to Northampton where she took up a position just south of the town and across the River Nene, here about forty yards wide. The front line of the archers built themselves a rudimentary stockade of sharpened stakes, an idea copied from Agincourt forty-five years previously.

It ran from west to east through the present goods-yard of the railway. From a loading ramp just inside the main entrance a good view is obtained of the area in which the battle was fought.

Warwick arrived up from London early in July with some four thousand men, spending the night on Hunsbury Hill. At dawn the Yorkists advanced against the Lancastrian position, crossing diagonally the present A43 from Towcester and then the present A508 from London, very near Queen Eleanor's Cross at Hardingstone. By the Eleanor Cross on 10 July 1460, the morning of the battle of Northampton, stood the Archbishop of Canterbury and the Papal Legate. They had come up from London to try and patch up a peace between Edward IV and Queen Margaret, wife of Henry VI. They were unsuccessful, but standing on the still existing mound, they saw the whole Yorkist army, now swollen to nearly 5,000 men, pass only half a mile away, on its way to attack the Lancastrians. These two elderly gentlemen, doubtless with a considerable retinue, must have been slightly apprehensive as to their safety, so close to the army of one of the great warring factions. Each could claim the protection of his cloth, but the Yorkish soldiery, or Lancastrians, would be unlikely to respect it if at all upset. One can visualize them hiding in the trees of Hardingstone Wood around the Cross.

Prince Edward's cavalry led the advance in pouring rain and when passing about where the present A43 and A508 cross, came under heavy arrow fire. The soaking ground made movement for the horses slow, but rain had already made the few and very primitive Lancastrian guns almost unusable, their charges frequently refusing to ignite. A pause, almost a stalemate, occurred. However, Warwick put his infantry in and round both flanks of the now halted cavalry and the advance was resumed until held up yet again by archery. (It seems odd that if the rain was so heavy as to render the guns almost useless, it did not also make the bow strings ineffective.) This pause in the advance was now brutally brought to an end by treachery in the Lancastrian line, as was not uncommon on both sides in the Wars of the Roses.

Lord Grey, commanding the right wing of the Lancastrian line, suddenly ordered his men to cease firing, and, walking out in front of his line, showed the leading Yorkist troops the gap he had made in the defence. The Yorkists poured through it and passing behind the remaining lines fired into them from behind. Few defending soldiers can stand such treatment and the Lancastrians, whose morale was never high, certainly could not. They turned and fled, and the enormity of the tactical blunder in taking up a defensive position with an unfordable river close behind them now became evident. The bridge, a narrow one only wide enough for one cart at a time, became choked and great numbers tried to swim the river, many drowning. King Henry was captured, probably having little idea of what was going on. Queen Margaret and her son, Edward, escaped to Scotland.

Nearly all the area on which the fighting took place is now covered with railway sidings. However, the approximate line of the stakes can be surmised from the loading ramp referred to. From the bridge the river is seen today to be entirely bounded by large factories. Even with the canalization that has taken place, the river is still thirty yards wide, and in 1460 was probably double that width though shallower. The line of advance from Hunsbury Hill diagonally across the two roads is entirely covered by a vast housing estate.

Queen Eleanor's Cross on its considerable artificial mound is easily found about two miles south of the bridge on the A508, the carving being in a remarkably good condition.

Eleanor's Cross today, at Hardingstone on the A.508 road. From the mound on which it stands, the aged Archbishop of Canterbury and the Papal Legate saw Yorkist troops only half a mile away *en route* for the Battle of Northampton.

EDGECOTE

Nine years later another battle of the Wars of the Roses, was fought in Northamptonshire at Edgecote, near Banbury. A substantial Yorkist force was encamped at Banbury but the two leaders, Pembroke and Devon, quarrelled about their billets. In a huff, Devon, the junior, took his men off to Deddington, while Pembroke took the Daventry road and camped on Danes Moor near Edgecote. Two days later Pembroke saw that during the night strong Lancastrian forces had occupied three hills surrounding his position. Instead of withdrawing westward out of the trap to rejoin Devon, he attacked the centre one of the three hills and captured it, and then turned left to attack the next, Culworth. Here he was repulsed and withdrawing to his camp took up a defensive position.

Some civilian toughs, collected by a violent Lancastrian supporter in Northampton, now appeared behind Pembroke's position. The main Lancastrian forces on their three hills, believing the new arrivals were proper soldiers, saw that the Yorkists were surrounded. All the Lancastrians advancing simultaneously, the Yorkists were cut to bits. Pembroke was executed with his younger brother, and Devon, with his forces from Deddington, arriving just too late to help, escaped to Somerset.

To see the battlefield, take the B403 Banbury-Daventry road. Four miles from the exit from Banbury turn right for Edgecote at the far end of Wardington. After two miles there is a large pond on the right. Another 200 yards farther, on the right, is a private drive leading to Edgecote Lodge. Great care is needed as this road is far from good. When you arrive at Edgecote Lodge where the road ends, you will see that it is a large farmhouse. The Farm Manager, Mr Hewson, will courteously allow the car to be parked in his yard and will show the

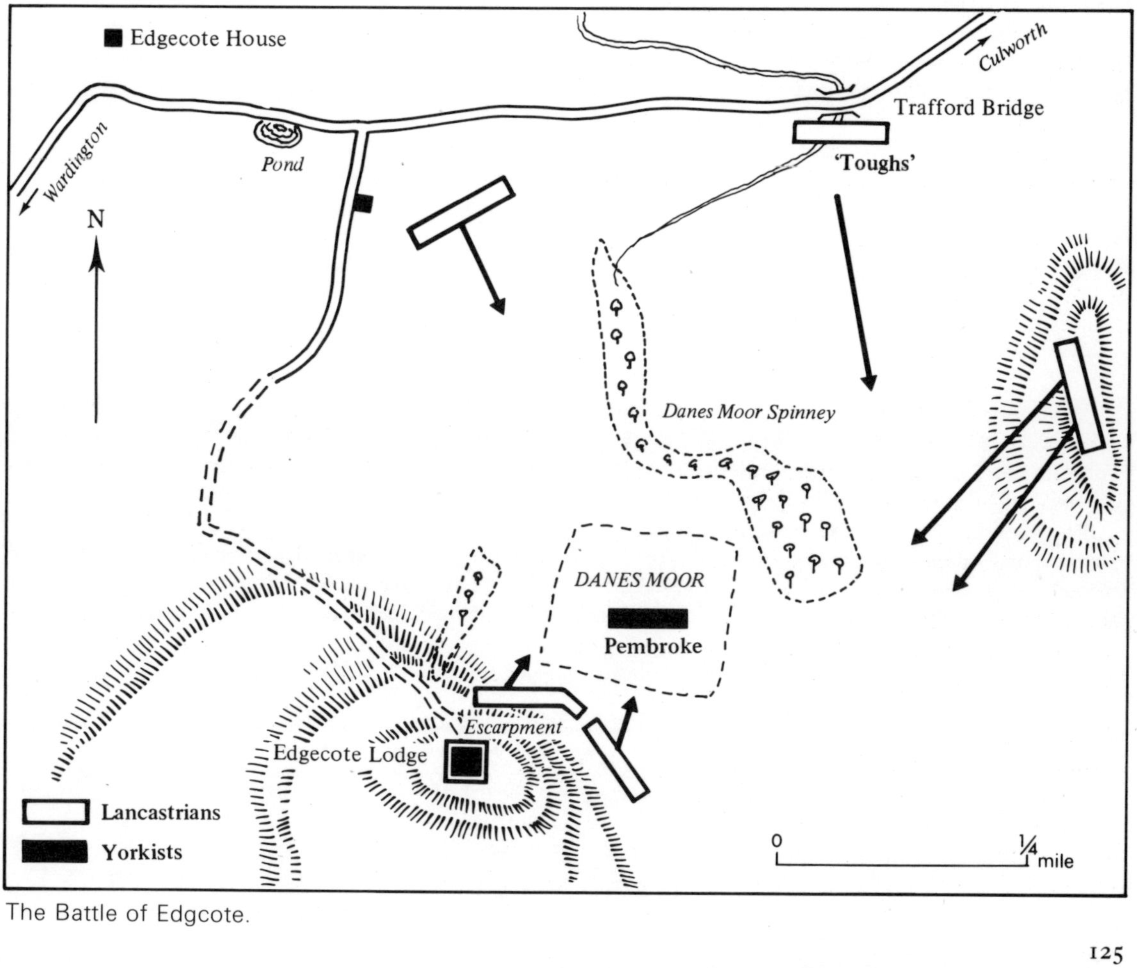

The Battle of Edgcote.

visitor down a very rough path towards the edge of a steep escarpment, less than 200 yards from the farmyard. Below is the field whereon the battle was fought, every inch of which can be seen eighty feet below, and no more than two hundred yards away. The hill on which the Lodge and the visitor are standing is clearly one of those originally held by Lancastrians. Across the field below and about half a mile away to the north-east is another, Culworth, held by them. The advance of the Northampton 'roughs', which so upset Pembroke's plans, was probably by Trafford Bridge nearby.

Mr Hewson pointed out to the author that the field below on which the battle was fought is called Danes Moor, and the spinney which acts as a backcloth to the scene is Danes Moor Spinney. He owns an old map which shows that on this very field in AD 822 or 892 – the date is so indistinct as to be uncertain – a battle was fought and the Danes were defeated by Alfred the Great's men as he cleared them out of England.

Of all difficult approaches to a battlefield, Edgecote is the most rewarding in the author's experience.

From the battle of Edgecote in 1469 nothing of military note occurred in Northamptonshire until 1643 in the Civil War. In this year Northampton town had declared for Parliament. Its already dilapidated walls needed much restoration work to withstand the three weeks' minor siege by Royalist troops. However, the walls were repaired and it held out; King Charles's soldiers withdrew and the town did not again figure in the Civil War. Like several other Midland towns it fared well under the Commonwealth, being a staunch supporter of Parliamentary government. But at the Restoration in 1660 its luck changed. The new Royalist government felt, not unreasonably, that a town that had been such a hot-bed of republicanism in the war, must never again be allowed to be dangerous, and Charles II ordered its walls to be demolished. The heart-breaking and back-breaking efforts of 1643 in restoring the old walls to withstand any siege by the Royalists were now to be reversed, and successfully. The townsmen worked so well that King Charles sent a special message of congratulations and thanks, and allowed them to use the demolished masonry for their own uses. Northampton in gratitude became almost Royalist in political thinking.

All Saints church built on the foundations of the vast church in which Henry I made his barons and bishops take the oath of loyalty to his daughter, Margaret, is perhaps the most conspicuous, certainly the most familiar, building in Northampton today. It stands in the centre, on an island site around which swirls unceasing traffic. High above the great portico stands a statue of Charles II and every year, on Oak Apple Day, a branch from an oak tree is placed on it.

THE BATTLE OF NASEBY

Two years after the little siege of Northampton there occurred one of the major battles of the Civil War, one of the decisive battles in British military and monarchical history, the Battle of Naseby.

The national, political, Royalist, and Parliamentary events leading to the Civil War have been outlined in the chapter on Warwickshire, wherein the first battle between Charles I and the Parliamentary forces was fought at Edgehill in 1642. In 1644 was fought the battle of Marston Moor, just, and only just, a victory for Parliament. The Parliamentarian troops performed so poorly that Cromwell formed his New Model Army, the chief characteristics of which were greatly tightened-up discipline, removal of inefficient officers, and increased and regular pay for the troops. The discipline and a new spirit were seen to advantage at Naseby, a year later, when King Charles was soundly defeated by this new army and, one must add, by the reckless and foolhardy handling of the Royalist cavalry by Prince Rupert, nephew of the king.

On 12 June 1645, old Tom Fairfax, commanding the Parliamentarian army, with Cromwell as second-in-command and commanding the cavalry, was near Daventry, Charles and his army being in and around Market Harborough. In the evening of 13 June the Roundhead main body had reached Guilsborough, while its advance guard had entered a small village, four miles farther north. There they surprised a Cavalier patrol feasting at an inn, and captured them. The village was Naseby.

The news of this incident reached the king in the middle of the night. By 6.30 a.m. the position from

The Battle of Naseby.

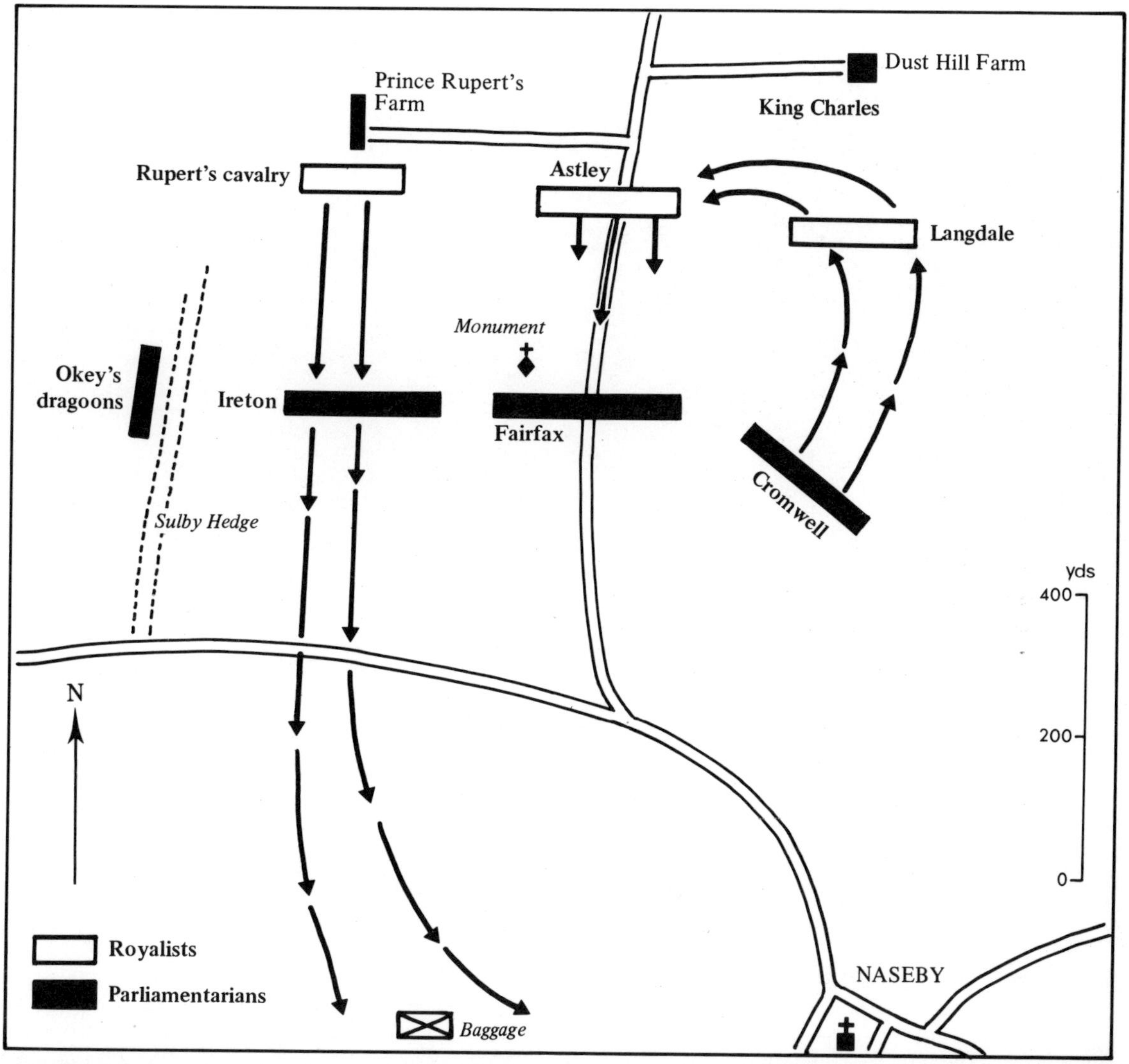

East Farndon to Oxendon was occupied, which, facing south, had the village of Naseby and the ridge in front of it in full view. About the same time as the Royalists were occupying the East Farndon ridge, Fairfax moved his main body forward, and occupied the Naseby ridge.

At about 7.30 a.m. Fairfax, accompanied by Cromwell, rode forward. He found the valley between the two ridges very boggy. He considered holding his present position, well down the ridge, covered by the bog, but Cromwell intervened. He pointed out that Rupert, out on the Royalist right flank, would almost certainly try to turn the position. It would be better to move the army back up the ridge and so tempt Rupert to attack across the valley, encounter the bog and finally have to charge uphill with his horses blown. Cromwell won the argument and Fairfax moved to the ridge behind him.

As in most battles in the sixteenth and seventeenth centuries, both armies were drawn up with a solid phalanx of infantry in the centre, forming an apparently immovable block. On the outer flanks were the cavalry, waiting to act as a reserve to come down on the flank or to harass violently an unsuccessful, hesitating or badly organized infantry advance. Rupert's cavalry was drawn up just to the west of the present Prince Rupert's Farm, while Langdale's left flank Royalist cavalry rested on the southern tip of Long Hold Spinney. The whole line covered nearly a mile. Charles's command post was at Dust Hill Farm.

Above Oliver Cromwell receiving his orders from 'old Tom Fairfax' at the battle of Naseby. From a painting by Charles Landseer.

Below Engraving of 1645 showing the disposition of the troops of Charles I and Sir Thomas Fairfax at the commencement of the battle of Naseby.

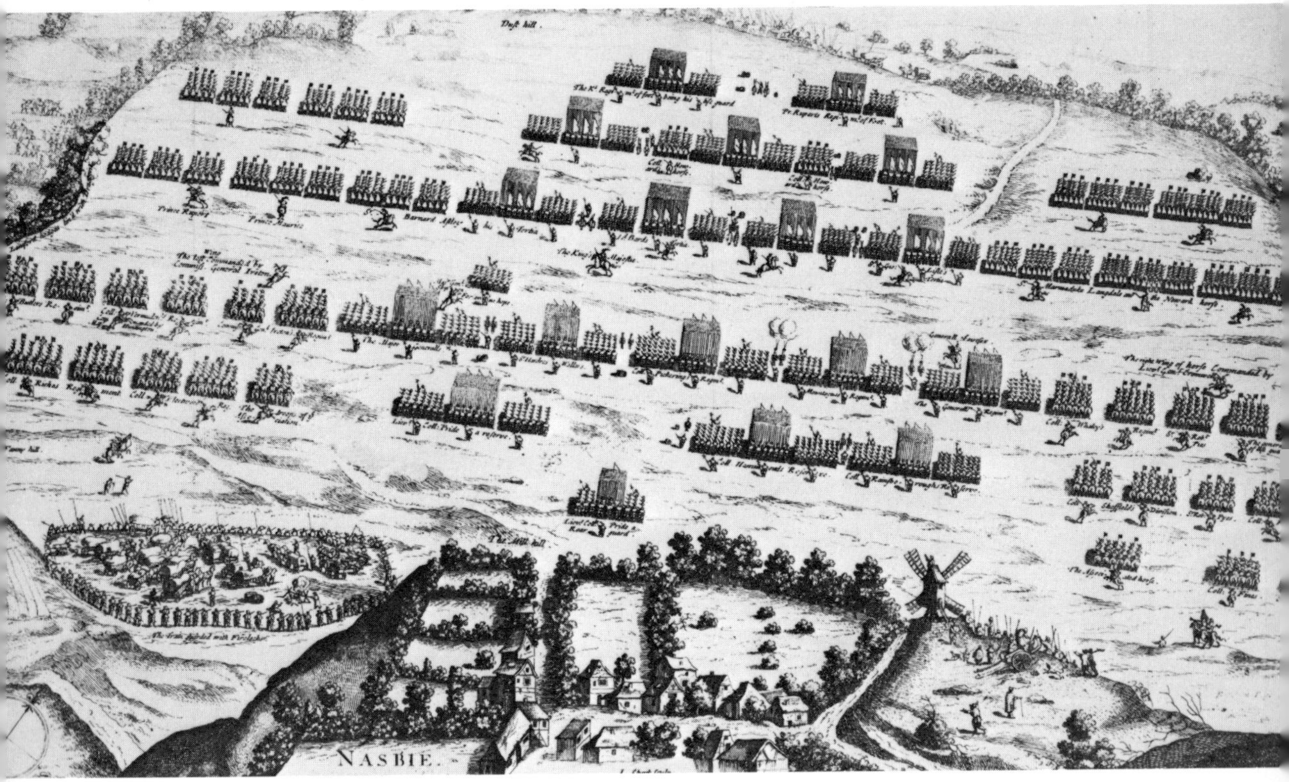

The table around which sat a Cavalier patrol when they were surprised by Roundheads the night before the battle of Naseby. It is now in Naseby church. A cavalier sword and stirrup are on the wall behind.

The Parliamentarians were drawn up in similar formation about a mile and a half away. Cromwell's cavalry on the right, owing to a sharp declivity in front of him, was slightly behind the general alignment – which was just behind Red Hill Ridge.

Out on his left flank and facing inwards, Fairfax placed 1,000 dragoons behind Sulby Hedge. It was admirably sited to enfilade Rupert's cavalry when they charged the Roundhead left flank – as they were almost certain to do – but if Rupert went very wide he could take the dragoons in flank, or worse still pass behind him. In fact Rupert passed in front of Sulby Hedge.

The battle of Naseby became the last major battle in British history in which artillery played no part. It became, as did most battles in the Civil War, largely a cavalry battle, the infantry playing their customary sheet-anchor, self-sacrificing role.

Rupert's blunder

Rupert persuaded Charles to order a general attack. Advancing slightly downhill from Dust Hill and into the depression, the Royal infantry started to ascend the opposite side. The Roundheads seeing the advance moved forward to meet it, and the two great masses of infantry were very near to each other. Rupert felt he too should now advance while all eyes were on the imminent infantry clash.

Given the order to charge, his horsemen passed outside the two infantry masses but kept inside the Sulby Hedge. From the dragoons there he received a ragged fire which did little damage. Gathering speed as he swept up the gentle slope he crashed into the left of the Parliamentary line about Red Hill Farm. The sword fight went in favour of the Cavaliers whose inbred and superior swordsmanship prevailed. Rupert gathered his men together into some sort of formation and resumed his advance, thereby committing one of the great tactical blunders of military history.

He galloped on for a good mile and unexpectedly came across the enemy's baggage-wagons parked in a small depression to the west of Naseby village. Rupert had difficulty in withdrawing his troopers from the plunder and it was almost an hour before he reappeared on the main battlefield, where much had been happening.

Rupert's reputation as a tactician is greatly harmed by this incident. He was serving no useful purpose whatever, and probably lost Charles the battle, his throne, and his life.

Meanwhile the Royalist infantry had pushed their opponents back to the crest of their ridge in a retreat that was beginning to have the aspect of a rout. Had Rupert been available with his cavalry to 'improve' this temporary victory the battle of Naseby would have become a Royal victory in two hours.

Rupert's early attack had defeated only half of the Roundheads' left-wing cavalry. The other half with

Above The battle of Naseby was fought in the light coloured fields to the left of this picture and the monument (to the battle) at the right is positioned at the centre of Fairfax's line.

Below Sulby Hedge at Naseby. Okey's dragoons were hidden here unknown to Prince Rupert whose unsuspecting troops passed inside the hedge and were subject to crossfire.

Ireton in command was intact. Seeing the infantry in the centre hard pressed by the Royalist infantry, Ireton advanced and wheeling to the right came straight into the open flank of Lord Astley's veteran infantry. The dragoons also advanced, from Sulby Hedge joining forces with Ireton, and together they firmly fenced in the Royalist infantry right flank.

Out on the Roundheads' right flank, Cromwell saw the left wing of the Royal Cavalry threading their way through furze bushes and broken country at the bottom of the hill below him. As they started to climb the rather steep rise he ordered his subordinate, Major Whalley, to advance with the front rank. The troopers thundered down the hill in superior numbers, the Royalist horse being swept from the field.

Whalley's men galloped on and almost reached Dust Hill, not far from King Charles's headquarters. There they halted, their horses blown, and they took no further important part in the battle.

Cromwell then wheeled his second and third ranks to their left and advanced in waves against the Royalist left. They were now beset on three sides and they began to give way.

Charles now had his last chance, the timely use of his reserve. But he did nothing and remained in observation on Dust Hill with his reserve for nearly an hour, watching a tragedy being enacted in the valley below him.

The Royalist infantry were practically surrounded, for some of Cromwell's horsemen had passed round to their rear. The regiments of foot laid down their arms one by one, ammunition expended. All had fought on to the end.

During this slow piecemeal surrender Rupert reappeared on the field. He would have liked to have put in a final charge, but his horses were past it.

His feelings must have been bitter as he, a hopeless eye-witness, gazed on the tragedy he had helped to bring about by his rash, pointless and ridiculous affair with the Roundhead baggage-wagons.

As the last regiment laid down its arms, Fairfax, regrouping his infantry began to move them forward, through the disarmed Royalists. The king saw that he had lost, turned and rode from the field.

The Royalists lost 4,000 infantrymen almost to a man and their twelve guns which were never used. Their cavalry too suffered, though not so heavily. The Parliamentary losses were heavy, especially among Ireton's cavalry and the infantry in the centre, but the total figure is not known.

Holmby House, Northamptonshire, where Charles I was imprisoned for a short time after his capture.

Charles flees

After Charles had ridden away, the whole of his baggage-train was captured. In it were found, among a mass of documents, incontrovertible evidence that he had been corresponding with foreign powers to persuade them to send over to England troops to restore him to his throne by force. This barefaced invitation to invade England, issued by the king, did more to convict him and bring about his execution than any of his other, and many, shortcomings as a constitutional monarch. The English have always been very sensitive to threats of foreign invasion or aggression and regard them with extreme distaste and worthy of supreme resistance. The invasions of the Romans, Saxons, Danes, and the Normans bred this determined patriotic attitude, and its force would have been felt by Napoleon and Hitler had either been so foolish as to try invasion. Had these documents not been found in Charles's train, there is little doubt that his inevitable capture and trial would only have ended in banishment, a potentially dangerous situation, or more likely incarceration in some English castle.

The battlefield of Naseby seems much changed since 1645. This is but an illusion, however, which is caused by a large number of simple hedges planted when the small fields were enclosed in 1830. Red Hill Farm, Prince Rupert's Farm, Broadmoor Farm, and Dust Hill Farm, each a group of buildings occupying a very small area only, have been built since the battle, and are of no interest to this story. In the seventeenth century, isolated farms such as are common today, did not exist in this part of England and all the workers, farmers, labourers, stockmen, etc. lived in the nearby village, a very tight little community.

Opposite This obelisk on the Naseby-Market Harborough road, though more imposing than that seen to the right of the battlefield, is a mile away from any scene of action in the battle.

Sulby Hedge still stands as it did in 1645 – for the most part two rows of trees some twenty yards apart growing on turf-covered banks. Towards its northern end it becomes only a single row – and the turf track between the hedges peters out. The steep declivity in front of Cromwell's cavalry is not so considerable as one might expect. The hollow in which Fairfax's baggage laager was hidden is quite clear but is less of a hollow than a falling-back of the ground down towards the western outskirts of the village.

But by far the most interesting things to see at Naseby are in the church. Here is the table round which the Royalist outpost was sitting, feasting, when surprised and captured by the Parliamentarians. For some years it was at the Inn, and later removed to the Manor House. Here, although treasured for many years, it was eventually discarded and turned out into the yard at the back of the Manor, exposed to the snow and rain of many winters. It now stands in the north aisle of the church, well worn, but restored. It is in quite remarkable condition.

Above the table is a sword picked up on the field, and one stirrup-iron. The sword has a few inches broken off its blade. These relics are naturally very darkly stained with rust and almost black, but the corrosion has been arrested and they too are in remarkable condition.

SOLDIERS OF NORTHAMPTONSHIRE

Unlike its close neighbours, Warwickshire, Lincolnshire, Bedfordshire and Leicestershire, the county of Northamptonshire was not called upon to provide a regiment for Charles II's new army, raised at the end of the seventeenth century, until 1740. In this year the 48th Foot was born, later to be the Northamptonshire Regiment and in the amalgamations of Cardwell in 1881 it was linked with the 58th (Rutlandshire) Regiment of Foot.

Each of the county regiments, the Regiments of the Line, have one or more battle honours of which they are mightily and justly proud. The Northamptons are no exception. The 1st Battalion, the old 48th, was at Fontenoy in 1745, all through the Peninsular War, gaining ten battle honours, and in the Crimea. The 2nd Battalion, the old 58th, was at the capture of Quebec, and Gibraltar, hence the castle as the main emblem in the Regimental cap badge. It went through the Peninsular War (five honours) and was in the expedition to New Zealand.

Opposite Officer of the 48th Foot which later became the 1st Battalion, the Northamptonshire Regiment. *c.* 1780.

Right The Earl of Cardigan leading the charge of the Light Brigade at Balaclava. His ancestral home is Deene Park, Northamptonshire.

It is a far cry from the Crimea War of 1854 to Northamptonshire. *Prima facie* the only connection seems to be that the 1st Battalion of the Northamptonshire Regiment – then the 48th Foot – arrived in the Crimea in time to take part in the siege of Sevastopol, arriving too late for the Alma and Inkerman, and that is all.

Charge of the Light Brigade

Perhaps the best known incident in British military history is the Charge of the Light Brigade at Balaclava in the Crimean War. The 'gallant six hundred' who rode into 'the valley of death' charged, at the gallop, the Russian guns. Starting with over six hundred cavalrymen, only one hundred and ninety-five survived and five hundred horses were lost. The Light Brigade was commanded by Lieutenant-Colonel The Earl of Cardigan, whose home was in Northamptonshire.

Cardigan's ancestral home since 1514 was Deene Park, ten miles north-east of Kettering, where he was born in 1797 and died in 1868. Immensely rich, extremely handsome, a superb horseman, and fantastically brave, he was also very stupid, very conceited, and ignorant as to how a senior officer should treat his subordinates. Convinced of overwhelming superiority over all his fellow-men, occasioned by his wealth and breeding, he believed he could do no wrong and that all men must inevitably subordinate themselves to him.

His treatment of his own officers when commanding the 15th Hussars was quite appalling and no senior officer was ever so much hated by his own officers. One of his despicable little tricks was to pay two of his own troopers from Aldershot to walk up and down St James's Street in dress uniform whenever he went to London so that he could be saluted, and be seen to be saluted, in mufti, every time he left his club.

Perhaps the worst example of his lack of interest in his subordinates was immediately after the Charge of the Light Brigade. Instead of leading the brigade, 'all that was left of it', back up the valley and reporting to the Commander-in-Chief, Lord Raglan, he left the field without a thought for his wounded officers and men and rode back to the harbour of Balaclava where his luxury yacht was lying. On board he drank a bottle of champagne and had a hot bath and dinner. His men rode back to their starting point and with no one to give them any orders, stood to their horses all night, without a meal of any sort.

He lived in great style at Deene Park where he entertained lavishly and overbearingly controlled his tenantry. Several souvenirs are in the house, including the hoof, now mounted as an inkstand, of his charger, Ronald, which he rode in the Charge of the Light Brigade.

He was married twice. His first wife died in 1858 – two years after Balaclava, and in the same year he married a most extraordinary woman, a Miss de Horsey. In her old age she was to become very eccentric. However, Cardigan was violently in love and shielded her from the world. He would never allow any man to hand her in to dinner either at Deene Park or when dining out, and arranged wild and extravagant parties to keep her amused, and in a good temper. She had been born in the reign of George IV and remembered going to a childrens' party at Buckingham Palace in the reign of William IV when about eight years of age. She died in 1915 at the age of 91, outliving Cardigan by forty-seven years. In her later years her eccentricity led her to have her coffin made, for which she had been measured and which she kept in the ballroom at Deene Park. She usually showed this macabre toy to her visitors.

In this account of the military history of Northamptonshire, a series of four set-backs to the county regiment in eighteen years at the end of the nineteenth century will be described. This account should in no circumstances be regarded as a reflection on the Northamptons but rather an example showing how the best laid plans can fail due to bad generalship.

Encounter with the Boers at Laing's Nek

In 1881 the 1st Boer War broke out, caused by the failure of the British government to honour its promise to give the Transvaal a greater degree of self-government and to remove the British regiments from the Boer's territory. The 58th, the 2nd Northamptons, were on ordinary garrison duty in South Africa, stationed at Mount Prospect, a tented camp three miles short of the southern border of the Transvaal, and near Majuba Hill.

Despite several requests by the Boer Republic (as they called themselves, although they owed and admitted allegiance to Queen Victoria) to London to implement its promise, nothing was done. In exasperation they invaded Natal astride the main Pretoria to Durban road, and the Northamptons, in camp with 60th Rifles and the Gordons, stood to.

The Boers took up a very strong position in the foothills of the Drakensburg Mountains around where the main road passed over the high ground at Laings Nek. General Colley decided to shift them and ordered six companies of the Northamptons with sixteen officers and four hundred and ninety men to attack the Nek. After a dusty march of four miles uphill the battalion deployed and started the very stiff climb, over deep dongas or water-courses. The colours were carried for the last time in action by any British battalion.

The Boers held their fire as usual and allowed the troops nearly to reach the crest of the ridge, almost breathless. Then they opened a shattering fire, killing the CO and the Second-in-command, and causing many casualties. The officer carrying the Regimental Colour was mortally wounded, the Colour being taken over by a sergeant, and farther up the hill the officer carrying the Queen's Colour fell in one of the dongas and broke his leg. Eventually the Quartermaster, coming up, carried both the Colours out of action as the Northamptons, totally unable to advance and suffering heavily from the fire of the almost unseen Boers, withdrew. As the troops retreated the enemy continued to fire and a number of men were shot in the back. A famous oil-painting by Lady Butler, exhibited in the Royal Academy in 1882, shows the Regiment retreating with two mounted officers from the Mounted Infantry Company galloping past, one calling to the other '*Floreat Etona*'.

Eleven days later came the battle of Ingogo. The 60th Rifles, with two horse-artillery guns went out to open up the main road up to Laings Nek and Pretoria. They crossed a ford in the River Ingogo on to a good fire position, on a plateau overlooking the road. At the far end was a large party of Boers whose superior marksmanship pinned the 60th down. Having successfully quietened the Riflemen they sent a strong party round their flanks to secure the ford by which the 60th and the two guns had crossed the river, now in spate. As darkness fell three companies of the Northamptons came up and extended the line of the 60th. The Boer fire died down, as torrential rain came on, and after a wretched night, the whole British force withdrew, one of the guns being lost in the river. The Northamptons had two men killed and four wounded.

Débâcle at Majuba Hill

Yet another eleven days after Ingogo came the battle of Majuba Hill. From Mount Prospect, General Colley led out a curiously mixed force of two companies of the Northamptons, two of the 60th and three of the Gordon Highlanders. Why Colley did not select one battalion for the task instead of parts of three, seems inexplicable. In Mount Prospect camp there were by now four complete infantry regiments available.

At 10 p.m. Colley led the six hundred men to the foot of Majuba Hill four miles away and started the steep, in places almost precipitous, six-hundred-foot climb in the dark, himself leading in tennis shoes. Half-way up he detached the two 60th companies, for no apparent tactical reason, and the remaining five companies reached the top at dawn, almost exhausted by lack of a night's sleep and a most strenuous climb in the dark, made worse by the heavy loads of entrenching tools, blankets etc.

A not very serious attempt was made to built a sanga-wall round the tip of the almost flat top but mostly the men and officers lay down to sleep. The Boers in their laager below saw movement on the summit and at once started a miraculous feat of field-craft. They climbed, now in broad daylight, the steepest side of this six-hundred-foot high massif, firing as they climbed upwards, at the red-coats they could now see lining the crest.

The British held their fire, although Lieutenant Ian Hamilton (Commander-in-Chief at Gallipoli thirty-three years later) suggested to General Colley that fire from above might not be out of place. The General refused his permission and the Boers climbed onward and upward. As they neared the top the British soldiers were at last allowed to fire but it was too late. The skill of the Boer marksmen in firing from behind rocks at close range kept the soldiers' heads down. Away on the northern sector of the almost circular position one company of the Gordons had no cover at all. The enemy saw this and sent a detachment of sixty picked men, all locals who knew the terrain, round the lower slopes to creep up close. The Highlanders lying in the grass would occasionally stand up and fire at some enemy far below them, quite unaware of the danger so close. Suddenly the Boers also stood up and fired a volley into the Gordons at point-blank range. Nearly all were hit, mostly killed, and the few survivors turned and ran back to the main position crying out that all were dead. This little panic spread to the other two Gordon companies who started to leave their positions. The successful Boers who had evicted the first Gordon company, now occupied their position and then started to fire into the backs of the Northamptons. These men seeing virtually all the Gordons now on the run, wavered too, and several of the younger soldiers in the battalion were affected in the growing panic and joined the fleeing Gordons.

A pause ensued for a while and Lieutenant Ian Hamilton again had the temerity to ask Colley if he could charge, as he knew the Boers, totally undisciplined as soldiers, could not stand against a bayonet charge. Again he refused. The officers of both the Gordons, and the Northamptons, tried to reorganize their lines and form a new defensive flank, but all the remaining men were now badly scared. Few could be persuaded to leave what little cover they had found, their morale had run out and it needed little more to make them join the stampede. An accurate burst of fire from the Boers brought the pause to an end, and most of the remaining troops on the top of Majuba turned and fled. A few of the stouter-hearted were taken prisoner, and General Colley was killed. It was said that he committed suicide, this being his third defeat by the Boers in less than a month. The Northamptons lost four

The last stand of the Northamptonshires at Saran Sar, 1897.

officers killed or wounded, and seventy-five men. One officer and thirteen men were captured.

The fourth set-back for the Northamptons occurred eighteen years later at the battle of Magersfontein, one of the 'Black Week' battles, fought in the last weeks of the dying century. Perhaps it is more accurate to call it a disappointment rather than a set-back.

The famous Highland Brigade just out from Scotland and with little active service 'know-how', was ordered to advance in mass by night for four miles over rough ground, and to attack the Boer trenches at the foot of Magersfontein ridge at first light. At dawn, and about to deploy from the ridiculous formation of mass into lines of attack, the Brigade was heard and dimly seen by the Boers in their trenches. Their devastating fire halted the entire brigade, the Brigade Commander and two COs were killed, no one knew anything and a complete stalemate occurred, made worse as the sun rose and the dark kilts and white helmets of the prostrate Highlanders were more clearly seen by the Boer marksmen.

The Divisional Commander, Lord Methuen – not a brilliant tactician – threw the Guards Brigade and the KOYLI round the right flank but they too were soon held up, and by midday the second stalemate occurred. Late in the afternoon the 58th, the Northamptons, and the Northumberland Fusiliers, went round the left flank. They advanced well and without opposition to within one thousand yards of the Boer right flank and were halted. Methuen realized that the failure of the Highland Brigade followed by that of the Guards showed that the position was impregnable and decided to call it all off. The Northamptons, anxious to avenge Majuba and the Laings Nek defeats of eighteen years ago, were bitterly disappointed, and there was much grumbling in the ranks as they marched to camp. Neither regiment in this little left flank attack had any casualties.

World War 1

In August 1914, the Northamptons were at Blackdown, part of the 1st Division. At Mons on 23 August the Division held the right of the British line, Northamptons being in the reserve brigade. On the night of the Battle of Mons the great retreat started, the 1st Division having only one brigade in contact with the enemy for several days. Although the Battle of Le Cateau was fought only six miles to the west, the right wing of the British Expeditionary Force simply marched.

On the 27th the Northamptons were on outpost duty covering the 2nd Brigade at Wassigny, when they saw a small party of German cavalry – Uhlans – advancing in reconnaissance apparently unaware of any British troops in the vicinity. The battalion opened fire and emptied two saddles. One German trooper was captured, sent to the rear, and his horse appropriated. The animal, now named 'Uhlan' by the transport men, remained with the Northamptons until the end of the war, giving excellent service and quite unaware that he had changed sides. At this outpost skirmish the Northamptons fired their first shots of the war, receiving none from the enemy in reply, and it was not until the evening of the 28th when a similar outpost fracas took place that a Lance Corporal was slightly wounded in the leg, five days after going into action at Mons. He was the Regiment's first battle casualty.

The 1st Northamptons remained with the 1st Division throughout the war, and finished active participation on 5 November 1918 at the village of Wassigny, where it had fired its first shots against Germans in August 1914 and captured Uhlan. The CO in November 1918, Lieutenant Colonel Robinson, had been a platoon commander in 1914 and his adjutant, Captain McNaught, had been Transport Sergeant.

The 2nd Battalion, from Alexandria, came home in September 1914, and was posted to the 8th Division, a newly formed division composed of regular battalions brought home from the Mediterranean, Egypt and the Middle East. It served with the 8th Division from November 1914 to the Armistice.

Territorials

The 4th Battalion, Territorial, was in the 54th East Midlands Division. This division served in the landing at Suvla Bay in Gallipoli, Suez Canal, the Palestine campaign, and then went to Egypt where it was heavily engaged in suppressing riots in Cairo over the Christmas period of 1918. After demobilization its final tiny little cadre, consisting of one officer and six men, did not reach Northampton until November 1919, four and a half years since leaving England, to be received at the Town Hall by the Mayor. Later the little party was entertained at Althorp by Earl Spencer, the Lord Lieutenant of Northamptonshire.

The Northamptonshire Regiment raised three active Kitchener's Army battalions, one, the 6th, winning four VCs. The 7th Battalion was raised and commanded by Edgar Mobbs, the famous rugby

international. Mobbs had gained a place in the history of international rugby football as an attacking three-quarter in one international match by jumping over the defending full-back about to tackle him. This incident so impressed the rugby football world that it was the subject of a well-known oil painting.

H.R.H. the Duke of Connaught inspecting the 1st Battalion, the Northamptonshire Regiment in France, July 1918.

The 2nd Northamptons in World War II had an outstanding world tour. Crossing to France with the BEF in October 1939, they took part in the evacuation of Dunkirk. After twenty-one months in the British Isles where they served in England, Ireland and Scotland, they took part in the landing at Madagascar, going on to India. Baghdad was followed by Suez, the Canal, the Sea of Galilee and Jerusalem, Sicily, Monte Cassino, Rome, then back to Egypt, Palestine, Syria including Beirut, Baalbec. Italy came next for a brief month and then, via Marseilles, to Belgium by train, and by foot to Hanover, Lübeck, the Baltic and the surrender of Germany.

Just before the Dunkirk evacuation, and when the whole country at last realized that not only was the 'phoney war' over but that the Germans would soon be in strength along the coast of Northern France, Mr Eden issued his call for recruits to join up and form the Home Guard, or Local Defence Volunteers as they were first called. The response was similar to that of Kitchener's call in August 1914 – 'Your King and Country need you'. With the utmost enthusiasm men rushed to enrol. Within a quarter of an hour of Mr Eden's announcement police stations were besieged either by telephone or by persons anxious to volunteer. Some arrived before the broadcast had ended. But the motives behind the response to Kitchener's call in 1914 and Mr Eden's in 1940 were deeply different. In 1914 the urge was to revenge the totally unwarranted invasion of Belgium. In 1940 it was to defend their own homes. In 1940 their country was in grave danger and Englishmen, seeing it, reacted violently.

All sorts of men volunteered to serve at once in the ranks as private soldiers. There were ex-RSMs and generals, holders of the VC, ex-officers who had been cashiered. Every arm of the services, including the Navy and the RAF were there. Their contempt for the enemy was as intense and sincere as it was dangerous.

The enthusiasm was shown by their unselfishness. They had no pay; all military training was after working hours and at weekends. They gained no material advantage at all except comradeship, but the slackers who were quickly allowed to resign represented less than 3%.

Battalions were formed by retired Regular Officers who had been rejected for recall to their regiments in 1939 as being too old for service with the new regular units then being raised.

In some outlying villages platoons often of thirty or forty men joined and the local officer would have farm labourers (who were exempt from normal military service) from eighteen years of age to veterans of sixty who had been sergeants, perhaps at Ypres, the Somme or Passchendaele.

Over 1,000 battalions were raised in England, Scotland and Wales during the four years to follow, the total strength in 1944 being 1,700,000. The men were largely formed and trained as infantry battalions, but about a tenth of the force were employed manning 140,000 AA guns, in coastal artillery or on bomb disposal. In 1943 women were allowed to join, being employed on clerical and signalling work, while a few of the younger ones actually assisted the gunners at the AA sites. Altogether 30,000 women volunteered.

The county of Northampton with a population of 400,000 raised fourteen battalions, at Peterborough, Warrington, Oundle (including one company of sixth-form boys from Oundle School), Kettering (two battalions), Wellingborough (also two), Northampton (also two), Daventry, Hardingstone, Towcester, and Brackley. Over ninety women served with these fourteen battalions, enlisted officially into the Home Guard.

Observation post of the 2nd Battalion Northamptonshire Regiment on the Anzio bridgehead, Italy, May 1944.

BEDFORDSHIRE AND THE COUNTY OF HUNTINGDON AND PETERBOROUGH

THE title of this chapter is unwieldy but correct. The two administrative areas are often spoken of as one and although possessing two separate identities are so similar and so small that they will be treated as one area for the purposes of this book.

The landscape is featureless and flat, except for the most southerly tip of Bedfordshire between Luton and Dunstable. Apart from the Great Ouse flowing through Bedfordshire neither county has any outstanding physical features, no mountains nor hills, no great woods, no marsh that might have promoted or retarded military operations.

The historian-traveller will find very few prehistoric hillforts, entrenchments, or ditches, and those which do exist are far younger than those built along the western frontier of England. One, Maiden Bower, one mile west of Dunstable, and just south of the disused railway track from Dunstable to Leighton Buzzard, is worth looking at. Its date is as late as *c.* 100 BC. It was used as a settlement as well as a defensive work, defensive not against a military aggressor but against local 'friendly' tribes, most of whom had their own similar defences against other tribes. The county of Huntingdon has very few prehistoric field monuments. Doubtless there were some but cultivation and later the brick industry has obliterated them. (Seven-eighths of the building-bricks used in England come from the two counties.)

Roman roads and settlements

The next period in history, the Roman occupation of England, has left little more for the travelling historian in the two counties than had the prehistoric era. There are however three interesting items to be seen.

Firstly the great Roman roads. On the west ran Watling Street and on the far east the modern A1 passes through Biggleswade and Sandy to join Ermine Street at Huntingdon. Between these two great roads lay a vast area where the agricultural and pastoral life went on as it had done, and was to do, for many centuries, little disturbed by the unceasing traffic on the two great ways.

Watling Street, the A5 London-Holyhead road, enters Bedfordshire to the south-east of Dunstable, and passes out some thirteen miles later south of Woburn. For several miles after leaving Dunstable the modern road lies precisely on the line of the original Roman road, and elementary excavation on the verges of the modern road where it is slightly above the level of the fields will disclose the original Roman foundations.

Passing the Punch Bowl public house on the A1 three miles out of St Albans towards Dunstable, and almost on the county border, the road runs dead straight. About a mile previously, however, the Roman Watling Street had for some reason diverged to its left and ran parallel to the present road and about fifty yards from it. A walk up a lane opposite the Punch Bowl will bring the visitor to two gaps in the hedges on either side. Standing in the western gap and looking out along the line of the ploughed furrows, you will see that the dark brown clay soil has a swathe of slightly lighter earth, and there is little doubt that this smear of beige on the darker brown is caused by the road metal of the Roman road just below the present ploughed field. This smear is absolutely straight, about twelve feet wide, parallel to the existing road and otherwise inexplicable.

On the other side of the two counties the A1 London-York road enters Bedfordshire just north of Baldock, and fifty-six miles farther on, passes out of Huntingdon at Stamford. On its way through Bedfordshire it passes through the little town of Sandy, seven miles east of Bedford. On its right or eastern side and just before entering the town, a large sandy eminence rises to 250 feet, covered with

Chesterton, Huntingdonshire. Mound and ditch of an unidentified prehistoric earthwork.

Watling Street, looking south east from Hockcliffe, Bedfordshire. The divergence at the Punch Bowl inn, referred to in the text, can be seen about three miles up the road.

thickly growing beech trees. This is Caesar's Camp, and round its almost flat summit and part way down the gently sloping sides can be seen the vague outlines of a Roman fort. The leaves from the trees have largely filled the trenches and, turning into humus and then soil, are obliterating all outlines. The trees prevent a general tactical impression being obtained. But overlooking the great main road less than a mile away, and with a considerable major stream, the Ivel, a tributary of the Great Ouse, flowing between the fort and the road, and presumably with no trees on the hill 1,700 years ago, Caesar's Camp made an extremely sound defensive position.

Fifteen miles north of Sandy the A1 passes through Godmanchester which, as its name implies, was an important Roman settlement and probably a posting-station for the Legions marching to garrison duty on Hadrian's Wall. For many centuries it was not known to be walled but in 1956 the digging of some deep sewer trenches disclosed traces of their foundations. Local archaeologists, aided by local subscription, a county grant, and encouragement from the Ministry of Works, then commenced digging and in many cases received permission from the owners to dig in back gardens. Results showed that a complete wall had surrounded the town following, as archaeologists so often find, the general line of the main streets of today. In Godmanchester the walls ran along what are today East Street, London Street, and The Causeway. Through the centre of the town runs Ermine Street, today known as The Stiles. There is clear evidence that the walls were built in AD 100-200, probably to protect the major buildings of the staging-camp against bandits. There is further evidence that much reconstruction of the walls was carried out in the fourth century, when some shallow ditches outside the walls were filled in and one single, more substantial, deeper and steeper tactical ditch was built, making a considerable obstacle for an attacker.

The battle at Biedcanford

Between the Roman evacuation of England in 415 and the Norman Conquest, Bedford springs briefly into military limelight in AD 571, the battle of 'Biedcanford'. For many centuries this name has been construed as the sixth century spelling of Bedford, and certainly four battles were fought between the invading Anglo-Saxons and the Britons within an area forty-five miles long, at Limbury, a northern suburb of Luton in Bedfordshire, Aylesbury in Buckinghamshire, Bensington and Eynsham in Oxfordshire. These five engagements, if Biedcanford is to be included, were fought within sixty-five years, and it is noteworthy that the unknown chronicler, admittedly writing 300 years later, mentioned the five names eastward from Limbury. This may imply an invader's gradual military progress from east to west. But there is no evidence that Biedcanford was Bedford – nor is there any evidence as to where in fact the battle was fought. All that can be said is that this almost unknown battle fitted into the pattern of the other four, both geographically and chronologically, and is supported in its claim to be Bedford by legend. Legends rarely have proof, but each one must have started at some time by people talking about some fact or other. Although often grossly distorted in the retelling through the centuries, the story mostly has some vestige of truth at its base. It is by no means impossible that Biedcanford was Bedford.

The earthwork at Water End, four miles east of Bedford on the A428 Huntingdon road and very close to it, is not easy to see as it is closely covered with small trees, and hidden by the hedge along the road. It is the only Danish field work known in the two counties, and its excellent tactical position points to its being a military outpost with visibility both ways along the road, doubtless only a track in the ninth century. It also overlooks a crossing of the River Ouse 400 yards away to the south and has a wide vista across the road to the north. The Danes mostly landed on the east coast and would, like all other invaders of England, move westward, pushing the defenders before them. Their progress in the face of Alfred the Great's magnificent defence and later aggression took some years, and periodic halts to consolidate gains were strategic necessities. Temporary defensive measures must have been taken during these pauses, and there is little doubt that the earthwork at Water End was an item in a wider plan. The Great Ouse was navigable up as far as Huntingdon in the Dark Ages, and it is probable that these Danes landed there.

Coming of the Normans

The coming of the Normans in 1066 threw the people of England into guerilla warfare yet again. There were no organized defensive troops to meet the invaders after Harold's army had dispersed at Hastings, yet the people were not defeated. The English had had much experience in resisting foreign troops, from the invaders who crossed the

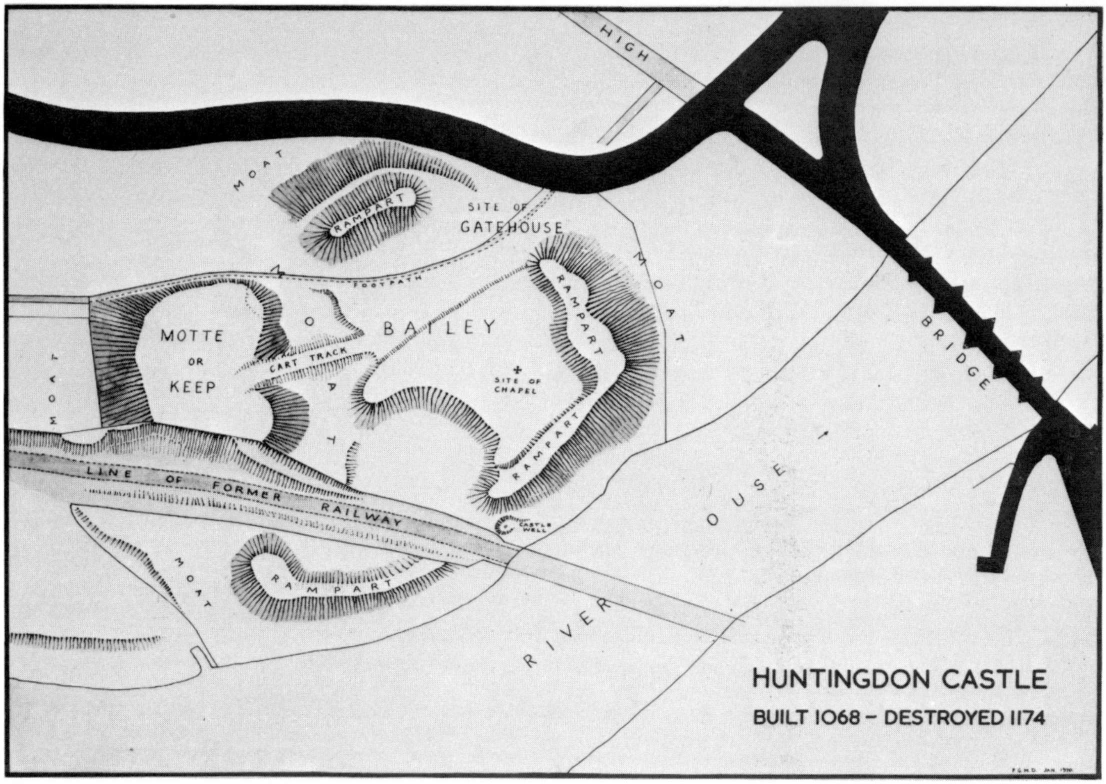

Plan of Huntingdon Castle, drawn from measurements made in 1970. The way to the keep via the gatehouse and embanked cart-track is described in the text.

channel and the North Sea after England became an island, followed by the Romans, Saxons, Danes.

The English tactics were much of the hit and run type. There was no central control, and organized Norman bodies were continually having to turn and face disorganized bands, led by their own chieftains. There were many ambushes, much cruelty, and many prisoners taken by either side never to be seen again. These marauding bands of Englishmen, patriotic to a degree, and only intent on harrassing the hated invader were a constant source of embarrassment to the conquerors.

Castles were built by the occupying forces to form strong points, refuges for hunted soldiers, rest stations, and stores for food and ammunition. One such castle was at Huntingdon, built in 1068. It is now in turf-covered ruins. It stands overlooking the Great Ouse by the thirteenth-century bridge which replaced a Roman one, and across which passes Ermine Street from London to York. The mound of the central keep is today some thirty feet high with a few fur trees on the top. There is a clearly defined secondary mound, lower than the keep, overlooking the car park and gardens of the Bridge Hotel, and it appears to have been a sort of outpost to observe the bridge. An interesting feature that remains is the little roadway from the barbican close to the car park up to the main keep, and within the walls. Between the barbican and the keep the roadway is carried on a three-feet-high causeway over the moat. It is, of course, entirely covered in turf but undoubtedly little digging would be needed to uncover road metal. Such must be there, otherwise the little causeway would have settled back into the moat in the passing centuries.

In 1215 Magna Carta was signed by King John at Runnymede. Great pressure was brought by the barons upon him to do so and he signed unwillingly, being very lukewarm in the promises given under his hand. Very soon after the signing ceremony he started to harass the barons individually, largely out of spite at having lost some of his almost unfettered liberties. The barons became so exasperated at his virtually going back on his signed word that in 1216 they invited Prince Louis, the Dauphin of France, later to be King Louis VIII, to come over with a party of mercenaries and fight with them against their king. Treason, if ever there was.

Bedford Castle burnt by Henry III

In October King John died and was succeeded by his son, King Henry III. At once Henry showed preference for the descendants of the Norman knights from 1066, placing many in country estates. Two of them, the brothers de Bréauté, were comfortably settled in Bedford Castle, a comfort which was not shared by the neighbouring countryside, to whom for eight years the brothers became a terror. They finally overstepped the mark in 1224 by imprisoning one of the king's judges. Three of the Justices were sitting in Dunstable, hearing cases of those ordinary people who had been dispossessed of their land by the two brothers. Thirty cases of unjust impounding were proved against the elder of the notoriously cruel brothers and consequently there was much jubilation in the town. The three Justices were celebrating a good day's work well done when word was brought that a posse of mounted men had left Bedford Castle to seize them. At once they separated but one of them, Henry de Braibroc, was captured and carried off to the castle.

This was too much for Henry. Although usually much in favour of anything a Norman might do, the seizure of one of the King's Justices was an insult to him, and at once preparations to besiege the castle and release de Braibroc were put in hand.

Much siege material was assembled at Bedford, some coming from as far off as Corfe Castle in Dorset. Men were recruited even from Lancaster and Newcastle.

Early in July all was ready for the siege, both inside and outside the castle, and for three successive days the king's official representative formally demanded the surrender of the castle and the release of the captive Justice. The younger de Bréauté, William, replied that his elder brother was the rightful owner, that only he could parley with the king and that he, Falk, was not in the castle and was in fact missing. Bombardment, by stones flung from slings, started immediately.

The castle was a rectangle, almost a square, with sides about 300 yards long. Its southern side rested on the Great Ouse River, but along the three remaining sides a moat deep and wide had been built with a substantial masonry curtain wall some five feet high on the outer bank. In the south-east corner and just inside the wall was the keep, an enormous artificial earth mound, twenty feet high with a diameter of eighty yards and faced with timber. On the western-facing main wall of the fortress was the barbican, the only way through the entire perimeter wall. It had been strengthened by the defenders with stones and building materials from the church of St Paul just opposite, which had been flattened.

There were four major assaults upon the castle, each after the artillery had made a breach in the walls. The second was by the barbican and allowed some soldiers to penetrate the outer defences and establish themselves in the inner bailey. The third brought the whole castle into the hands of King Henry's men, with the exception of the keep, which remained impregnable for some days. This was finally reduced by the royalist soldiers pushing wheeled carts filled with inflammables up against the mound. The timber baulks on the sloping keep sides were set on fire, as was the main building on the mound; de Bréauté's men surrendered and the King of England's flag was run up on the flagstaff.

Henry de Braibroc, escaping from the flames and the attempts of some of the defenders to murder him, got out, bringing with him Falk's wife, and some soldiers captured with him at Dunstable nine weeks before.

Next day eighty-three people, including William de Bréauté and all the knights, retainers, and men-at-arms serving in the castle were hanged on gallows close by the keep, only the chaplain being allowed his life.

Falk de Bréauté was eventually captured and Henry showing great, perhaps undeserved, mercy, allowed him to escape to France where he lived for some years before being poisoned and buried in a pauper's grave.

Today only the base of the great keep of the castle remains. It is completely circular, and, the only original earthwork now remaining, it appears like a gigantic truncated sugar loaf. The top of the mound is turfed and used as a bowling green, said to be the oldest green in England.

The small moats on the north and east side still remain as a public flower-garden covered by well-kept lawns and flowering shrubs. Immediately beyond the eastern part of the moat runs Newnham Road. About 100 yards along the western boundary of this road is a surviving section of the curtain wall of 1224. It is still five feet high in a few places and is well worth inspection and photography.

All other traces of the curtain wall by the keep have disappeared and the main walls of the castle are now buried deep underneath the modern shops and houses. St Paul's Church has been rebuilt twice and is a magnificent edifice in a splendid position, facing where the barbican originally stood.

Moated farms

All over the map of Bedfordshire are examples of 'moats', usually by isolated farms, suggesting that these were originally surrounded by a defensive ditch, or with a 'keep' close-by to which the farmer's family and servants could withdraw on the approach of danger. The author counted over thirty moats on one sheet of the Ordnance Survey map of Bedfordshire. One of the largest is 300 yards from Birchfield Farm, near Great Barford, on the Bedford to Huntingdon Road. It is roughly rectangular, about eighty yards each way, and the 'island' within the moat could hold many humans and their animals. The moat itself is today five feet deep with gently sloping sides, but six hundred years ago must have been eight or nine feet deep. This obstacle to assault would have been of little use however without some sort of wooden stockade built on the inner lip of the moat behind which the women and children could shelter from arrows or stones. To dig this moat at Birchfield Farm and then to erect the stockade must have been a tremendous task. Surprisingly the moat is overlooked by higher ground only 200 or 300 yards away, on two-thirds of its perimeter. Another easily-found moat is at Astwood, on the road from Bedford-Newport Pagnell road. It is much smaller than that at Birchfield Farm, and is almost circular with a diameter of twenty-five yards. The ditches are deeper, the sides steeper and its tactical position better. It commands an excellent view northward. It lies behind the first building of the farm first on the right on entering Astwood from Bedford.

The Wars of the Roses scarcely touched Bedfordshire or Huntingdon and certainly no incidents, large or small, are recorded. But in 1588, a hundred years after the Battle of Bosworth, England was threatened by the Spanish Armada. Although geographically and psychologically, so far from any apparent danger in this quiet corner of England, Bedfordshire was ready to defend her country and provided forty cavalrymen and their horses, and five hundred infantrymen, who paraded before Queen Elizabeth at Tilbury. A thousand pounds in cash was subscribed – a very considerable sum in those days.

Cromwell

The Civil War found Bedfordshire and Huntingdonshire largely Parliamentarian. The great families, as in most other counties, were fairly evenly divided and sympathies were by no means passionately for one side or the other. Such comparative apathy is understandable in a county that had little industry, much agriculture and only a few great houses to lead society or maintain a remnant of feudal overlordship. The Earl of Bedford, whose son was to be the first Duke of Bedford, showed his own impartiality by fighting for Cromwell at Edgehill, and for King Charles at 1st Newbury. But indirectly Huntingdon town played a great part in the Civil War. Oliver Cromwell was born there. He attended the local school, now a Cromwell Museum, and lived in the town until the age of twenty. During his late teens he was an undergraduate at Cambridge sixteen miles away, and not until he graduated did he go to London to begin the parliamentary career, which led to his becoming Dictator of England and its greatest soldier-politician. The house where he was born was demolished many years ago but the present one on the same site was built of materials from the original. The garden is preserved. All Saints church where Cromwell was christened in 1599 was rebuilt in 1620 but the font has been preserved.

With the death of Cromwell in 1658 all military events within the two counties ceased until World War II.

Opposite Plaque on the site of Cromwell's birthplace.

Above Cromwell House, on the east side of High Street, Huntingdon. A much later house built on the site of, and with materials from, the house where Oliver Cromwell was born.

The Grammar School, Huntingdon. A Norman building much restored. Oliver Cromwell attended the school here *c.* 1610. Samuel Pepys, the great diarist, was also educated here.

THE BEDFORD REGIMENT

In 1688 and 1702 two military events occurred directly concerning the two counties, the raising of the 16th Regiment of Foot, later to be the Bedfordshire Regiment, and the 31st, to be the Huntingdonshire Regiment.

The Bedfords were in Marlborough's great army which, in 1704, marched from Holland to the battlefield of Blenheim. More than 350 miles were covered in six weeks over execrable roads, the men's boots being far from comparable with the present-day ammunition boots. There was little sickness, no looting (strictly forbidden by Marlborough and rigidly enforced) and no desertion.

The great march completely surprised the French who imagined Marlborough and his army to be in Holland. They went on the defensive at the village of Blenheim, and the 16th Foot, the Bedfords, in the leading line of the right-hand brigade earned their second battle honour, Blenheim, one of the decisive battles of the world.

In nearly two hundred years between Malplaquet and South Africa in 1900, only two battle honours came the way of the Bedfords – Surinam and Chitral. In Canada in 1814 and 1815, however, the Regiment was sent for to return immediately to Europe and meet Napoleon's new threat on his escape from Elba. But the transports arrived late and the Bedfords did not arrive in Europe until a month after Waterloo. This incident, following on the long gap in battle participation since Malplaquet over a hundred years before, gave the Regiment the nickname of 'the Peacemakers', a most unfair name. A regiment serves where it is sent, and often a long stretch of garrison duty in some out-of-the-way place where nothing seems to happen is a tribute to a Regiment's reliability, an indication that it can be trusted.

Raising of the 16th Foot, later to become the Bedfords, at Reading in 1688.

Overleaf The Bedfords crossing the brook before Nebel, near Blenheim, 1704. Note the men have their arms at the slope and are not extended.

Battle of Moodkee, 1845. Advance of the 31st Regiment, then the Huntingdonshire Regiment, later to become the 1st East Surrey Regiment and linked with the 70th Foot from Glasgow.

World War 1

In August 1914 the 1st Battalion in the 5th Division from Ireland was present at the battle of Mons, and at Le Cateau three days later. Here it was in the front line in an excellent fire position covering the Cambrai-Le Cateau road. The low banks between pasture fields from behind which the Regiment fired all day can still be seen. Rifle and machine-gun fire caused enormous casualties to the Germans who were quite unable to advance across the road. But the units on the two flanks had to withdraw and the Bedfords were ordered to retire and leave their perfect position. The retirement was the beginning of the great Retreat from Mons, and the Bedfords were to march, tired out after their wonderful day at Le Cateau, 134 miles in nine days.

About sixty per cent of the men in the ranks and the junior NCOs were reservists, called back to the colours on mobilization. They were not as fit as the serving regulars, and the long and continuous marching, the unaccustomed army boots, the very hot weather and the scarcity of hot food caused much distress. GHQ ordered the baggage from the wagons to be jettisoned and badly exhausted men to be carried. To have fallen out or collapsed by the wayside must have meant capture by the Germans, but the Bedfords marched on, not taking advantage of the concession to put some men on the wagons. From the day after Mons, 24 August, to the end of the Retreat, 6 September, only thirty men of the Bedfords fell out all of whom rejoined later, none being taken prisoner.

The 1st Bedfords remained in the 5th Division throughout its active service career, including going out to Italy in October 1917 – after the Italian disaster at Caporetto – until recalled to France in March 1918 to meet the final great German offensive.

The 2nd Battalion was in the famous 7th Division, joining it on returning home from Pretoria on the outbreak of war. It took part in the 1st Battle of Ypres in October 1914, and in September 1915 was in the 7th Division's successful attack at Loos. In December the 21st brigade, with the 2nd Bedford unit, was transferred to stiffen the 30th Division with which it remained for the remainder of the war.

Carrying a casualty of the 1st Bedfordshire Regiment from a trench near Beaumont Hamel, 1 July 1916.

The 5th Territorial Army Battalion, from Bedford, Dunstable, and Luton, served with the Home Counties Territorial Division and took part in the battle of Suvla Bay in Gallipoli, remaining with the division in Egypt and Palestine. Three 'Kitchener's' Battalions were raised in Bedfordshire, all serving in France.

Although the county of Hertfordshire is not within the subject of this book it would be unfair not to mention the Hertfordshire Regiment, a Territorial Battalion affiliated to the Bedfordshire Regiment, and, in 1914, virtually its second Territorial Army battalion. It was one of the earliest Territorial battalions to go out to France (November 1914 after just three months embodiment) where it was posted to the 4th Guards Brigade. It did so well in such splendid company that it was nicknamed 'The Herts Guards' and remained with the Brigade until the formation of the Guards Division in August 1915. Transferred to the 39th Division, it maintained its high standard throughout the war. In 1919 in recognition of its achievements the title of its parent regiment was changed to The Bedfordshire and Hertfordshire Regiment.

THE HUNTINGDONSHIRE REGIMENT

The Huntingdonshire Regiment, the 31st Foot, had a curious career. It was raised in 1702, fourteen years later than the Bedfords, and had a magnificent collection of battle honours, among others seven from the Peninsular War, and five from India. It had fought at Fontenoy where in the centre of the front line of battalions between the Scots Fusiliers and The Kings it suffered very heavily, losing 133 officers and men killed, including its CO, and 141 wounded. In 1777 it was serving in America and was in the British defeat at Saratoga. This victory enabled America to implement her independence, declared the previous year, from Great Britain. It is typical of American chivalry that the 3,500 British soldiers captured as prisoners of war at Saratoga were allowed to pile arms and march away.

In 1881 the British Army was reorganized as far as its infantry regiments were concerned, and the 31st Huntingdons were joined to the 70th Foot, the Glasgow Lowland Regiment, and given the title of the East Surrey Regiment. It is not clear why a regular regiment based in the East Midlands should be linked with a Lowland regiment from Scotland and then given a territorial designation from south of London. But this extraordinary proceeding completely severed the 31st Regiment's connection with Huntingdon and so it passes beyond the scope of this book.

Another curious event in the military life of Huntingdonshire occurred in February 1914. A completely new Territorial battalion, The Huntingdonshire Cyclist Battalion, was raised.

In early 1914 all the existing Territorial battalions throughout the Army were of long standing. Most of them had sent out volunteer reinforcements to their respective Regular battalions in the South African War and now bore 'South Africa 1900–1902' on their colours. Very few could not claim an existence of eighty years, and the reason for suddenly raising an entirely new Territorial battalion at this particular time seems obscure.

It could not have been because of a sudden threat of danger from over the Channel. August 1914 was still six months away and there was not a cloud in the international sky, other than the Kaiser's bombastic boasting.

Possibly the people of Huntingdon suddenly realized that they had had no local soldiers or units of any sort, Regular or Territorial, since their own 31st Foot had become the East Surreys. Lord Roberts's stirring call for conscription, with his slogan 'Wake up, England', in 1910 had probably planted the seed but it is still odd that three and a half years were to elapse before the county acted.

For some reason, the new Huntingdonshire Cyclists did not go overseas between 1914 and 1918. They were, of course mobilized on 4 August, as were all the other Territorial units in the country, but served, mostly on the East Coast, on defensive tasks, throughout the war. They were finally disembodied in April 1919, since when the only military representatives in Huntingdonshire have been the public schools' OTC.

World War II

The Bedfordshire Regiment's two regular battalions were overseas for most of World War II. The 1st Battalion, in Egypt, served in the desert, at Tobruk, and with Wingate's Chindits in Burma. The 2nd Battalion was at Dunkirk, Algiers, and Monte Cassino in Italy. Two Territorial battalions of Bedfords were in the 18th Division sent out as a last hope to save Singapore. The attempt failed and the whole division was captured by the Japanese. One-third of the men, building the Burma Railway, died in captivity.

The Regiment was amalgamated in 1959 with the Essex Regiment to become the 3rd Battalion, The Royal Anglian Regiment.

The Home Guard

Bedfordshire, though such a small county, raised seven battalions of Home Guard from 1940. The Northern Sector had battalions at Bedford (three), Biggleswade, and Ampthill, with headquarters at Bedford. The Second Battalion in the Northern Sector, based on Biggleswade, had 2,300 men enlisted and serving by 1944. This battalion had 1,854 effective modern lethal small arms. They included Lewis guns, Sten guns, automatic rifles, and Browning machine-guns. In addition anti-tank rifles and mortars were 'on the strength'.

One old soldier in this Biggleswade battalion had joined the Bedfordshire Regiment in September 1914, in response to Kitchener's call. He served on the Western Front from 1915 to 1919, when he was demobilized. In 1940, aged almost forty-six, he was engaged in his civilian occupation of farming when again he heard the call, this time from Mr Eden for the Home Guard. He joined the following morning, and at once recruited 100 men in his parish, naturally being the platoon commander. Later he became the Company Commander, a position he held until the Home Guard 'stood down' in 1944.

In 1952 Whitehall thought another national emergency was approaching and decided to re-form the Home Guard. This old soldier was asked to take command of the new Biggleswade battalion, although now aged fifty-eight, and he commanded until 1957 when the Home Guard was again disbanded.

This by now elderly officer, Lieutenant Colonel F. Vincent, still farming today, organizes an annual Home Guard Officers' dinner and from his mailing list of thirty ex-officers he usually gets an attendance of fifteen or twenty. He was awarded the OBE in 1966, not only for his service with the Home Guard, but for fifteen years' service as Chairman of the Milk and Dairy Produce Committee of the National Farmers' Union. He is a typical example of an asset that Great Britain has enjoyed for many decades, and still enjoys, a civilian who is at heart a soldier.

The two Home Guard battalions in Biggleswade were not the first on the scene. In 1803 when the menace of an invasion by Napoleon was considered imminent a certain Major-General Harvey of Ickwell raised a local troop of horse-artillery in the village of Northhill, Colonel Vincent's village, from men from the surrounding villages. It remained active and prepared until after Waterloo. In Northhill today there is a group of cottages called The Barracks, where it is believed these horse-gunners of 1803 were billetted.

The Southern Sector had three battalions based on Luton (two) and Dunstable. The Luton battalions were much implicated in enemy air raids searching for the many factories and railway-yards there. The men were constantly being called out to help the Civil Defence to clear the lines and streets, and to prevent looting. The latter activity was so quickly and roughly dealt with by the Home Guard that it soon became unprofitable and went out of fashion.

Huntingdon, the second smallest county in England, raised three battalions of the Home Guard in 1940-4. The 1st was based on Huntingdon, the 2nd came from St Ives and its immediately surrounding villages. The 3rd Battalion was spread out over a large agricultural area, with thirty-two outlying platoons, between St Neots and the Bedfordshire border, and to the east, as far as the Cambridge border. Within ten months of the call in May 1940 by Mr Anthony Eden, 940 men had joined this widely spread 3rd battalion, a broad average of thirty men from each village. Two years later the total topped 1,100 men.

Like all Home Guard battalions half-day, whole-day, and week-end exercises were carried out by this 3rd Battalion after elementary and individual training had been completed. They were greatly enjoyed by the men and junior officers who thus got a feel of what field operations would be like in darkness and in all kinds of weather. One such exercise in this Battalion, on a Sunday, was held in appalling weather, and the men had just been dismissed to their homes, about 6 p.m. Two hours later it was necessary to call the battalion out again to round up four German airmen who had baled out of their plane. All were caught and the excitement of actually chasing, and catching, a real enemy made this Sunday's exercise the best ever held, despite the weather.

As was often found in the Home Guard battalions, communications between companies and battalion headquarters and between different battalions was one of the greatest problems. The 3rd Battalion tried carrier pigeons. Eight amateur fanciers in St Neots, and three in nearby villages co-operated and training of the birds and the times they made were most satisfactory and efficient.

The Huntingdonshire Sector, in addition to the three battalions referred to also had two battalions in Peterborough. The railway line and junction there was even more important than at Luton, although Peterborough has less than half the population. Here constant watch against saboteurs was always necessary, and even until 1944 a permanent unchanging roster of sentry duties was necessary and maintained.

When the Huntingdonshire Home Guard stood down in September 1944, the county could muster 4,500 men and 87 women in the three battalions under arms.

Overleaf 2nd Battalion Bedfordshire and Hertfordshire Regiments passing through Cesena, Italy. 24 October 1944.

INDEX

Numbers in italics refer to captions